SOUTHERN REGION THROUGH THE 1960S

Year By Year

MICHAEL HYMANS

AMBERLEY

First published 2017

Amberley Publishing
The Hill, Stroud
Gloucestershire, GL5 4EP

www.amberley-books.com

British Library Cataloguing in Publication Data.
A catalogue record for this book is available from the British Library.

ISBN 978 1 4456 6642 6 (print)
ISBN 978 1 4456 6643 3 (ebook)

Typeset in 10.5pt on 13pt Sabon.
Origination by Amberley Publishing.
Printed in the UK.

Contents

Preface

My previous book charted the changing face of the Southern Region through the 1950s, from recovering after the Second World War through to the implementation of the Beeching Report.

The 1960s was another decade that witnessed major changes to the network. For the passenger, rather than the enthusiast, there were major improvements, especially on the line from Waterloo to Bournemouth, where noisy, smelly steam locomotives were replaced by quieter, cleaner, more reliable electric trains.

Branch lines that survived the cuts were served by new diesel multiple units rather than the tank engine that could have been well over fifty years old. These were more efficient and were the saviours of many branches.

For the enthusiast, however, it was a terrible decade. Many branch lines throughout the Southern closed and with them the last of classes of locomotives dating back to LBSCR, SECR or LSWR days disappeared.

1967 saw the last main line steam locomotive leave Waterloo for Bournemouth. The Bournemouth Belle also ran for the final time: shed masters who were also steam enthusiasts made sure it was steam-hauled rather than operated by the diesel traction that had taken over the service.

The demise of steam also led to dwindling numbers of enthusiasts armed with cameras and notebooks on the end of main line platforms.

The 1960s saw an improvement in many families' finances and this in turn led to commuters abandoning the railways in favour of private motor car, while cheaper flights saw families flying to Spain rather than travelling by train to South Coast resorts for their annual holidays.

One ray of sunshine though was the growth of preserved railways, with the Bluebell Railway leading the way and being a source of inspiration to the Kent & East Sussex, Mid-Hants and Swanage Railways.

Chapter 1

1960

Class 33 Diesels

The first of the Type 3 diesels started to be delivered early in the year. They were Bo-Bo 1,550 hp engines built by the Birmingham Railway Wagon & Carriage Co. Ltd and not dissimilar to the Type 2s already delivered to the Eastern and Scottish Regions. They differed in one respect, in that they incorporated electric rather than steam heating equipment. This meant that the water tank needed for the latter could be omitted, allowing a larger eight-cylinder engine to be fitted, thus leading to an increase in power. An advantage of electric heating was that when heating was not required, as on summer passenger or freight trips, then extra power was available for the traction motors. Eighty-nine locomotives were ordered, with the last thirteen being built to the Hastings gauge. They were introduced to replace all the steam locomotives remaining on the Eastern Section of the Region.

Royal Ascot

All the special trains run for Royal Ascot were designated as first-class only. They were formed of Portsmouth line electric stock, upgraded simply by the addition of antimacassars. In the past, any extra units needed for the event had been stored, awaiting their return journeys on the Up line between Ascot West and Ascot signal boxes, but this year they were stabled at Woking, Chertsey or Windsor. Steam specials arrived from a variety of places including Llanelli, Wolverhampton and Nottingham.

Ferry Services

The British Transport Commission (BTC) announced that all Channel Island ferry services would be moved to Weymouth from Southampton from May 1961, although opposition from the latter was expected. The seasonal trade in tomatoes from the Islands needed seven freight trains daily to places such as York, Crewe, Cardiff and Nine Elms. To add to congestion problems at the docks, the quay at Weymouth was prone to flooding at high tides.

A general seamen's strike affected British Railways' ferries in August, which brought sailings from Southampton to a halt. The *St Patrick* continued to sail from Weymouth, which resulted in extra trains being laid onto the port. At Newhaven, British Railways' steamers were cancelled but the French laid on extra ferries to cope with the demand and at least one special train was run to take strike-bound passengers from Southampton to Newhaven. Another special went to Gatwick Airport with passengers who were due to sail for America on the *Queen Mary*.

The *Caesarea* (which had been launched in January 1959) made its maiden commercial crossing from Weymouth to the Channel Islands on 2 December. The vessel and its sister ship the *Sarnia* both had sixty-six berths in private cabins, as well as sleeping lounges for other passengers. In November, around 200 press and other invited guests had been entertained to lunch on board the vessel between Weymouth and Southampton as part of a large publicity drive for the new 'one class' service that was due to start in May. It was hoped that the new service would win back some of the passengers who had turned to travelling by air to the Islands. The lucky guests had been taken to Weymouth by first-class Pullmans *Juno*, *Alicante*, *Daphne*, *Cassandra* and *Niobe* and it is thought that this was the first occasion that Pullmans had travelled on the Quay tramway.

The *St Patrick* was undergoing a £30,000 refit to bring her up to the standard of the other vessels on the route. Three steamers that used to operate out of Southampton had been made redundant – *Isle of Jersey* had been sold, *Isle of Sark* was awaiting disposal, and *Isle of Guernsey* was being held in reserve.

Floods

The worst floods in living memory occurred at the end of September and throughout October. The West of England bore the brunt in the early days with many branches being forced to close on more than one occasion, but the chaos moved eastwards over the ensuing weeks. Expresses from Waterloo had to be terminated at Exeter Central, which rapidly became congested.

Rules in place at the time prohibited diesel-electrics from running over tracks where water had reached a level of less than an inch from the top of the running rail. Emergency running was allowed, however, at 3 mph until the water levels reached 4 inches over the top of the rails. Diesel-hydraulics were permitted another 2 inches before they too had to stop operating. Steam was not subject to these restrictions, so on many occasions diesels had to be replaced by steam to carry on over flooded tracks.

On the Central Section it was November before the flooding caused any serious disruption. On the 3rd, the 06:41 Eastbourne–Tunbridge Wells service arrived at Rotherfield with only one carriage attached. The other two had been hit by a landslide at Argos Hill and had been left stuck in the mud. The train could not progress any further due to flooding between there and Redgate Mill and passengers had to transfer to buses.

Uckfield was also under water but passengers could not be transferred to buses as the bus garage too was flooded. Perhaps the most serious flooding occurred at Lewes. A local stream had become swollen and burst its banks. It first flooded the

Brighton–Eastbourne main road before coursing through the cattle market and breaking through a wooden wall, inundating the station area with water levels nearly reaching the top of the platforms. With all tracks through the station being electrified, this brought services to a standstill. A variety of steam locomotives and coaching stock were eventually pressed into service and an emergency service was run. It took two days before the water levels fell to less than 4 inches over rail level when a Hastings six-car diesel unit was used for the Brighton–Eastbourne service.

The Kent & East Sussex Railway (KESR) also suffered from flooding the same weekend, with the track between Salehurst and Rolvenden suffering severe damage: an estimated time of four weeks was given to effect repairs.

Further flooding occurred on the Somerset & Dorset Railway on 4 December when a landslip at Midford caused the closure of the line to through traffic until 10 December. Radstock shed was under water and all locos on shed were steamed with a view to evacuation, but it never came to that.

Bluebell Railway

The Bluebell Railway ran its first train in August, while BR were still operating services over electrified lines into Horsted Keynes station, so their first trains only ran as far as Bluebell Halt, about 400 yards short of Horsted Keynes station. As there was no run-round facilities at the halt, trains had to be topped and tailed with A1X No. 32655, repainted in London Brighton & South Coast Railway (LBSCR) livery and renumbered 55 *Stepney* at one end and ex-SECR P Class No. 31323, later named *Bluebell*, at the other end.

Accidents

At 14:58 on 28 January, a collision between three passenger trains occurred at Borough Market Junction. The 14:22 electric multiple unit (EMU) from Hayes to Charing Cross had left London Bridge on a clear signal but overran the next signal, which was at danger. It hit the passing 13:00 Hastings–Charing Cross diesel-electric multiple unit (DEMU) as the two lines converged. The impact, although at low speeds, derailed the leading coach of the EMU towards the Down Slow line, where it was immediately hit by the 14:35 Charing Cross–Tattenham Corner EMU. Seven passengers were injured, though fortunately none seriously. The fire brigade and police were quickly on the scene and within 35 minutes the passengers had been de-trained and escorted back to either London Bridge or Borough High Street. The wreckage of all three trains was cleared overnight and damage to track and signalling was repaired, allowing rush-hour traffic to operate normally the following morning. The driver of the 14:22 EMU was blamed entirely for the accident as it was deemed that he had gone through a red light.

Another accident happened in South London at 06:26 on 1 April in thick fog at Herne Hill Sorting Sidings. The signalman had forgotten he had a light engine stationary at a signal when he released the electric locking of the block section and accepted a Down passenger train into the same section. This train hit the engine at about 35 mph, pushing it 80 yards along the track. The impact destroyed the cab and killed the motorman. Those passengers requiring hospital treatment had all been taken away by 07:16. The wreckage was cleared during the course of the morning and normal running resumed just after midday.

Waterloo was the scene of another accident at 18:32 on 3 June. The 18:18 steam-hauled express to Weymouth had left Platform 12 late at 18:31. It had only travelled 280 yards when its fourth carriage was struck a glancing blow by empty electric stock heading for Platform 6 that had overrun a red signal. Neither train was derailed but both were extensively damaged, although there were no serious injuries. The express stopped at Vauxhall where the passengers alighted, catching various trains back to Waterloo to restart their journeys. The electric train was towed away and both lines opened within two hours of the collision. The motorman was blamed for the collision as it was deemed he had passed a signal at danger.

On 8 April, the Battersea to Three Bridges freight became derailed north of Horley, causing passenger services to the South Coast to be terminated at Redhill or diverted via Dorking and Horsham to Three Bridges, where they had to be reversed for their onward journeys.

New Locomotives

The new diesel shunter programme planned for 370 nationwide, with only nine bound for the Southern (Nos D2287–95).

Locomotive Movements

During the summer, new Class 33 diesels had ousted steam power on some 'Man of Kent' services from Charing Cross to Folkestone.

Ex-South Eastern & Chatham Railway (SECR) D Class 4-4-0 No. 31737 was taken to the British Transport Commission's museum at Clapham, housed in a former London Transport bus garage. The first part of its journey involved being towed from Ashford to Nine Elms before being jacked-up onto a Pickfords' low-loader for its onward journey through London's streets.

An unusual visitor to the Region was No. D5513 on a football excursion from Shoeburyness to Southampton Central. It took its stock to the New Docks to await its return trip and is believed to be the first main line diesel to enter the docks.

On 29 January a Brighton Belle unit was used on a Waterloo–Portsmouth special in connection with the launching of *Caesarea*, the new steamer for the Channel Islands service.

In 1959, LMR Black 5s were banned from the Mid-Sussex line, so the first excursion to Bognor in 1960 was in the hands of No. D5074.

Between early July and September, Butlins Expresses ran on Saturdays from Victoria to Bognor at 09:58, with a train in the opposite direction leaving at 10:29.

They were not advertised but ran non-stop between the two termini using a 4-COR with prominent blue roof boards.

After extensive relaying of track on the Lyme Regis branch, LMR 2-6-2T No. 41297 was trialled over the line initially with only a brake van in tow, before operating a return trip from Axminster with two carriages.

Line Closures

The Rye Harbour branch closed on 29 February, while goods services were withdrawn from Poole to Poole Quay on 2 May.

Last of Classes

The Southern's Locomotive Condemnation Programme of 1960 planned for the scrapping of 206 engines, which would mean the demise of the L, T9, O1, 0415, 0298, P, E1(0-6-0T), G6 and R1 classes.

Miscellanea

There was some confusion as to which way the new lion on wheel emblem should face. In most cases it had been applied with the lion facing forwards on both sides of the engine, but the College of Arms stated that the lion should always face left, so it should be facing rearwards on the right-hand side of tenders.

On 6 December, a Plymouth–Brighton train came to a halt at Shoreham when the crew realised the tender was devoid of water. The crew tried to replenish it with a hose attached to the mains but it proved to be inadequate. Eventually the fire was dropped onto the track, which promptly set fire to the sleepers, and the local fire brigade were called to douse the flames. The farce got worse when the fireman dropped his shovel onto the conductor rail, which caused a short-circuit. The following train was a Bognor–Brighton EMU that became isolated. Behind that was a Cardiff–Brighton steam-hauled train. The loco from that was sent forward to pull the EMU back wrong line to Lancing, before rejoining its own train. Meanwhile, buses provided a replacement service for passengers.

During the year, large orange 'V's were painted onto one cab end of the Hampshire and Hastings DEMUs. This was because these units only had one guard's van as opposed to one at either end of the steam-hauled stock they replaced, with the guard always riding at the rear. The 'V' denoted that this was the end at which the guard's van was located, so that any postmen waiting on stations to load the mail could see as the train approached where they should be waiting to load the train and ensure minimal delay. Later, when yellow warning panels were painted onto cab fronts, this 'V' was changed to black.

The first Automatic Warning System (AWS) in the region, which gave an audible warning inside the cab if the next distant signal was 'on', was installed between Basingstoke and Exeter.

A new car-by-rail service was introduced between Surbiton and Exeter, where cars were driven into wagons while their owners travelled in accompanying carriages.

A new depot for imported fruit and vegetables was opened at Hither Green. It was capable of handling complete trains arriving from the Channel ports and could store up to 200,000 tons of produce annually. With customs on site, it could cut the time for produce to reach shops by up to 24 hours.

On 4 January, the push and pull services between Eastleigh and Andover were replaced by three-car DEMUs.

Vandalism was becoming a problem, albeit not so much as on other regions. The Southern had suffered £11,000 worth of damage to rolling stock in the first three months of the year. This compared with an annual rate over the entire network of £500,000.

In August the BTC issued a directive that all withdrawn locomotives must be offered for sale whole to scrap merchants to save labour at their plants; however, although cutting up ceased for a while at Eastleigh, it soon resumed.

In December a Bill was published that proposed doing away with the BTC and replacing it with four Boards for railways, canals, docks and London Transport. Road haulage would be run by independent companies. Railway regions would become autonomous and be able to control their own charges. Of the £1,600 million of debt owed by the railways, £400 million would be wiped out. The railways would then be expected to pay their way within five years.

At the end of 1960, stock on the Southern consisted of 1,119 steam, 177 diesel and 27 electric locomotives, as well as 4,088 EMU and 216 DEMU carriages.

C Class No. 31004 was fitted with a snowplough when photographed at Ramsgate on 18 February. It was to be withdrawn in November 1961.

Another C Class was No. 31268, pictured in unusually clean condition at Ashford on 5 February. This was one of the last survivors of its class, lasting until April 1962.

No. 31634 was a U Class mogul looking good in mixed traffic lined black livery with the later British Railways insignia on the tender. It is pictured at an unknown location on 9 February 1960.

0-6-2T No. 32503 was a Class E4 built by R. Billinton for the LBSCR in 1900. It was originally numbered 503 and named *Buckland* before being renumbered 2503. It had a long life, being withdrawn in April 1963.

The crew of No. 30584 pose for the camera at its normal haunt of Lyme Regis on 1 June 1960.

Ashford on 7 July 1960 and Class C No. 31218 was on its home shed of Ashford.

One of the cleanest Q1 0-6-0s you are ever likely to see was No. 33027, on shed at Ashford on 20 April 1960.

Ex-GWR 0-6-0PT No. 9620 was one of the engines brought in as bankers for the Folkestone Harbour branch. It is seen here at Ashford on 11 April 1960.

Some of the A1Xs owe their longevity to the severe weight restriction over the Langstone Viaduct on the Hayling Island branch. No. 32678 is seen here on the island on 18 September 1960.

Two images that are not strictly Southern but ran within the region. The miniature railway at Hastings ran a scale model of GWR Saint Class No. 2943 *Hampton Court* (above), and on the world's largest miniature railway, No.7 *Typhoon* at New Romney on 2 June 1960.

4-6-0 No. 30860 *Lord Hawke* on a Bournemouth to Birkenhead express in the summer of 1960. (Courtesy Ben Brooksbank)

No. 30800 *Sir Meleaus de Lile* waits to leave Weymouth Town with an express to Waterloo. (Courtesy Ben Brooksbank)

M7 No. 30105 grabs the attention of two young trainspotters at Bournemouth Central on 6 June 1960. (Courtesy Ben Brooksbank)

No. 34045 *Ottery St Mary* pauses at Basingstoke on a Bournemouth–Newcastle service during the summer of 1960. (Courtesy Ben Brooksbank)

Ex-LMS Fairburn 2-6-4T No. 42081 leaves Rotherfield and Mark Cross heading south on the Cuckoo line towards Eastbourne during 1960.

E4 No. 32515 at Hailsham, also heading south on the Cuckoo line during 1960.

Chapter 2

1961

Kent Coast Electrification

The third rail between Dover and Folkestone (Central and Harbour) was activated on 1 May, as was the power between Sevenoaks and Pluckley. Two weeks later the section between Maidstone West and Paddock Wood went live, followed by Folkestone Central to Ashford a week after that. Full working by EMUs started on 12 June when fifty CEP and BEP and fifteen HAPs became available. On the same date, sixty D65XX and twenty-four E5XXX locos were due to take over freight workings from steam. This second phase of the Kent Coast Electrification Scheme had been brought in twelve months ahead of schedule, although the signalling had not yet been converted to colour light, enabling faster times to be achieved.

The scheme had involved electrifying 132 route miles, which needed thirty-four power sub-stations and a new control room at Paddock Wood. Ashford and Folkestone Central stations had to be completely rebuilt and new carriage repair shops were built at Chart Leacon near Ashford.

Seventy steam engine drivers from Tonbridge, Ashford, Dover and Stewarts Lane underwent an intensive three-week course to learn to drive diesels. This brought the total number of men capable of driving diesels to 380, of which 144 could also drive electric locos.

New E6XXX Locos

The first of these versatile locomotives was due to be delivered by the end of the year. They used power from the third rail when it was available, but also had diesel-electric engines for running over non-electrified lines. The initial order was for six engines (Nos E6001–E6006).

One early proposal was for the diesel engine to be as powerful as other main line diesel locomotives, but this was dropped since there would be no reduction in running costs and fitting two powerful engines would mean building larger locomotives.

The engine chosen was a 600 hp engine already being used in DEMUs, which provided twice as much power needed for normal shunting requirements. The electric motors would provide greater power than a Type 3 diesel – up to 40 mph – but this advantage would then decrease as speed increased. This new locomotive would be capable of running in tandem with other diesel-electric locomotives or with EMUs. The bodies were kept within 8 feet wide, so running over the restricted Tonbridge to Hastings line was possible.

Channel Island Services

Fog over the Channel Islands grounded all flights on Good Friday so the ferries were extra busy over the Easter period, with *Caesarea* carrying a capacity load of 1,400 and the reserve vessel, *Isle of Guernsey*, making an appearance. This was not her only appearance as she substituted for the new vessel *Sarnia*, which was late being delivered.

Sarnia docked at Weymouth for the first time on 13 June after bringing a party of guests from Southampton. These lucky guests then continued their outing back to Waterloo on a train of Pullmans. *Sarnia* made her first commercial voyage on 17 June. On 14 July she ran into a quay in the Channel Islands during bad weather. She was not badly damaged but her return trip to the mainland was delayed by around eight hours.

The service in general was not going well. The ferries often arrived late at Weymouth. Further delays were then experienced on the tramway between Weymouth Quay and Weymouth Junction, resulting in the train losing its path and a late arrival at Waterloo. There were calls to move the ferry service back to Southampton or risk losing more passengers to air services.

Steyning Line Centenary

The line celebrated its centenary on 7 October with A1X No. 32635 in LBSCR Stroudley's yellow livery on show in the yard of Steyning station. Both Steyning and West Grinstead stations were decorated for the event and trains were strengthened to four coaches to deal with demand, with E4 No. 32468 making two round trips. It had been cleaned especially and carried a small commemorative headboard.

Bluebell Railway

Adams Radial Tank No. 30583 (Class 0415) ran light from Eastleigh to Brighton on 9 July before making its way to Sheffield Park, where, that evening, it worked a return trip to Horsted Keynes.

The first passenger train to work into Horsted Keynes station took place on 29 October. The Bluebell's four-coach Chesham set was used with the Class 0415 and an A1X at the front and two Class Ps at the southern end. At this time there were 137 condemned coaches stored between Horsted Keynes and Ardingly.

Accidents

At 09:18 on 20 March, the 08:33 EMU from Addiscombe to Cannon Street consisting of six heavily laden coaches ran through a red light and collided with an empty twelve-car DEMU leaving for Grove Park. The leading coach of the EMU struck the eighth coach at an angle before hitting the end of the ninth coach, tipping that and the following coach onto its side. The front two coaches of the EMU were derailed but stayed upright. Eleven passengers and the motorman were slightly injured. All four tracks between London Bridge and Cannon Street were blocked and all services had to be re-routed to other London termini or stopped short. The wreckage was cleared overnight and normal services resumed the following day. The motorman admitted that he had mistaken a green signal on an adjacent track as being his and was found solely to blame for the accident.

A similar accident occurred on 11 April at 17:26 when another EMU passed a red light approaching Waterloo and hit a West Country 4-6-2 running light tender first to Nine Elms. The motorman's cab was crushed and he was unfortunately killed. Emergency services were quick to respond but the accident happened on a viaduct, making access to the wreckage difficult. A local businessman supplied a mobile crane to lift firemen and ambulance crews from street level to the tracks. Fourteen passengers and staff needed hospital treatment but they had all been removed from the scene within 45 minutes. All were released the same day.

The front two coaches had telescoped to a depth of about 6 feet and the loco's tender derailed. Considerable disruption was caused with power to Platforms 1–7 having to be turned off. The wreckage was cleared overnight and normal services resumed the following day.

Waterloo continued to have problems when, on 3 May, shortly after 09:00, an empty EMU, 4117, derailed between Platform 1 and the down carriage sidings. Repairs to the track were not finished until the evening, necessitating the cancellation of all evening rush hour trains to Shepperton via Kingston and stopping trains to Epsom.

On 15 September at West Street crossing, between Hythe and Marchwood in Hampshire, a car driver failed to heed the road sign warning of an ungated crossing ahead. When he saw the road over the crossing was clear, he thought it safe to proceed. Unfortunately the 08:06 a.m. Fawley to Southampton passenger train was approaching and by the time the car driver saw the approaching engine it was too late. The engine, which was running tender, struck the car on the front nearside. There were four occupants in the car. The man in the front passenger seat had seen the train bearing down on them and had opened his door and tried to escape, but was tragically crushed between the car and the train. The other three occupants survived with minor injuries. The driver of the car stated that he was a stranger to the area and that the windows of his car were shut and they were all chatting, which may be why he had not heard the engine's whistle.

19 September saw a minor accident outside Brighton when the 11:28 from Victoria collided with some empty coaching stock. Although there were no injuries, the main

line was blocked and all London-bound services had to be diverted via Hove or Lewes. Delays were heavy and Brighton station was besieged by day-trippers wanting to return to the Capital, so twelve buses had to be run non-stop to East Croydon in an attempt to clear the backlog.

Loco Movements

The Reading–Portsmouth service was dieselised on 1 May using Western Region DMUs.

No. D2292 was fitted with a bell for working the Weymouth Tramway. It was trialled on 6 and 7 April, hauling the maximum loads of forty-five wagons or twelve bogie carriages, which it coped with.

The last regular steam-hauled boat train via Chatham was the 09.30 on 25 March and was in the hands of No. 34077 *603 Squadron*.

On 8 July, No. 20003 operated an excursion over the entire length of electrified track along the South Coast between Portsmouth and Hastings. It achieved this by being pulled backwards into Brighton from Preston Park by a steam loco before continuing its journey eastwards. At Hastings it then took its empty stock to Ore carriage sidings.

An impressive sight on 7 July was a pair of Class Cs, No. 31583 and No. 31714, in charge of a pigeon special from Newcastle, which consisted of two passenger coaches and seventeen bogie vestibule vans. They had taken over the train at Dalston East Junction. The return journey was even more spectacular (if less successful), as the handbrake on one of the vans had been left on. The pair struggled as far as Lewes, where they were put into the goods loop, and the errant vehicle, that now had very flat wheels, was detached. The pair continued but had been damaged and they were relieved at Three Bridges. Both engines stayed at Three Bridges for about a week before being taken to Ashford Works, where they were both withdrawn.

An engine making its way to private ownership at a flour mill was P Class No. 31556, which ran light from Brighton to Robertsbridge on 14 June where it was met by its new owner, who named it *Pride of Sussex*.

Line Closures

The last day of normal working on the Hawkhurst branch was on 10 June. Five coaches were needed to cope with the demand. C Class 0-6-0 No. 31588 had to replace the usual H Class rostered to the working. An LCGB excursion traversed the line the following day and the nine coaches required double-heading by O1 No. 31065 and C No. 31592. Many wagons and vans were still in yards along the line, requiring further loco movements to clear them.

11 June saw the last passenger train over the Kent & East Sussex Railway. It was a seven-coach enthusiast's special in the hands of two A1Xs: No. 32662 at one end and No. 32670 at the other. The climb into Tenterden proved too much for the pair

of Terriers and a stop of several minutes had to be taken to allow sufficient steam to be raised to complete the climb.

The Westerham branch closed on 28 October. The usual two-coach push-pull set could not cope with the crowds wishing to travel over the line one last time, so a seven-coach set, 277, hauled by No. 31737, was called into action. With limited run-round facilities at Dunton Green, Q1 No. 33029 was needed to haul the set back up the branch. Several round trips were made, with the last one being at 20:30.

Two societies had been formed to try to save the line – The Westerham Branch Railway Association and the Westerham Valley Railway Society. These two joined forces in 1962 to become the Westerham Valley Railway Association and looked into whether the line could be run voluntarily for use by commuters on weekdays and for enthusiasts at weekends. They were offered the line by BR for £30,000 on the proviso that a commuter service was run. This would mean that BR could stop having to subsidise the local replacement bus service, which cost them £8,700 p.a. The Association was granted a lease on Westerham station and later Brasted station. However, BR then changed its mind and demanded that the line was purchased for £53,000 instead of being leased. With the help of an anonymous donor, the Association were able to offer £30,000 for the whole track, together with the land and buildings at Dunton Green, which BR accepted. Unfortunately, the backer's plans for redevelopment at Westerham station were turned down and he withdrew his backing. BR then began talks with Kent County Council regarding sale of land to enable construction of the M25, and any hopes of saving the line were extinguished.

The Association had agreed to purchase H Class No. 31263 and some ex-Metropolitan Railway carriages that had been stored at Dunton Green station. When the project failed the coaches were sold to the Keighley & Worth Valley Railway and No. 31263 went to the Bluebell Railway.

Passenger services to Winchester Chesil ended on 11 September. The station had only been re-opened for the summer and used on Saturdays only for short journeys from Southampton to avoid congestion at Winchester City. It had lost the through service in March 1960.

The 5-mile Turnchapel branch from Plymouth Friary was closed to all traffic on 30 September – ten years after the end of passenger services. It served communities in the eastern part of the city at Lucas Terrace Halt, Plymstock and Oreston.

Passenger services from Grain ended on 2 November, with the last train being the 11:37 consisting of a two car push-pull set coupled to H Class No. 31324.

The Allhallows branch closed completely on Sunday 3 December, with the last passenger train being the 20:38 consisting of seven coaches hauled by C Class No. 31689.

Last of Classes

The E/E1 4-4-0 , E1/R 0-6-0T, H15 4-6-0, P 0-6-0T, D1 4-4-0 and O1 0-6-0 classes disappeared from the Southern, with the last P and O1 examples going for preservation.

Shed Closures

Dover (73H) shed closed in October. At the time of closure it had seven ex-GWR 0-6-0PTs allocated to it for banking boat trains out of Folkestone Harbour. A few weeks before, a couple of E6 tanks, Nos 32410/5, were homed there and earlier still in the year it could still boast seven BB/WCs.

Hither Green (73C) closed in the same month as Dover. It was still home to five C Class 0-6-0s introduced in 1900. Seven W Class 2-6-4Ts had been allocated to the shed until their withdrawal in May earlier in the year.

Miscellanea

The first part of the National Transport Museum opened in an old bus garage at Clapham on 29 March. No locomotives were on display at the time, just a collection of models, maps, tickets and other ephemera. An admission fee of 1/- (5p) was charged.

The large concrete coaling plant at Stewarts Lane started to be dismantled in 1961.

A pair of A1Xs, Nos 32650 and 32646, working the Hayling Island branch on 12 July 1961.

King Arthur Class No. 30798 *Sir Hectimere* reverses out of Waterloo to be refuelled at Nine Elms before its next journey on 6 April 1961. It originally worked on the Eastern section so would have been fitted to a six-wheeled tender, but was given an eight-wheeled variety when switched to the Western section, where it had to work longer routes. It was withdrawn in June 1962.

An unidentified electro-diesel E6XXX was on a freight from Eastbourne running through Hampden Park when photographed here.

On 11 June 1961, Class 01 No. 31065 and Class C No. 31592 operated the *South Eastern Ltd*. They pulled the trip from Paddock Wood to Hawkhurst and then back to Tonbridge.

The *South Eastern Ltd* then continued from Tonbridge to the KESR behind H Class No. 31308 and D1 No. 31749, where a pair of A1Xs topped and tailed the train over the light railway.

The down Golden Arrow with No. E5015 in charge as it passes through Folkestone Junction.

King Arthur Class N15, No. 30800 *Sir Meleaus de Lile*, sits on the ash pit at Dover in 1961.

4-4-0 D1 No. 31727 was withdrawn in March 1961 after a long life. It was introduced as Class D No. 727 in 1901 for the SEC by Wainwright. It was rebuilt in 1922 when it was given a superheated Belpaire boiler by Maunsell. In Southern days it was renumbered 1727 before finally becoming No. 31727 under BR.

E4 No. 32556 was a R. Billinton design of 1910 for the LBSCR. In later life it found its way west and worked at Southampton Docks prior to being withdrawn in October 1961.

No. 32337 was a K Class built in 1913 for the LBSCR. The well-loved class of seventeen engines were all withdrawn at the end of 1962.

A scruffy-looking Schools Class No. 30915 *Brighton* on a train of vans at an unknown location in 1961.

Chapter 3

1962

Dr Beeching

On 15 March, Dr Beeching, in a speech to the National Association of British Manufacturers, proclaimed:

> The railways will never be a good sound business unless we do some very drastic pruning. There would have to be a great deal of closures. The main routes are cluttered up by stopping services and consignments of small freight.

Later in the year, in a speech to the RCTS, he said:

> There is no doubt that pruning of little-used services is essential. This will enable us to make better use of the railways' most valuable asset – the trainload movement of dense flows of passenger and freight traffic at speed over long distances. Far too much money is being lost on uneconomic stopping services for which railways are no longer the right answer, and by the use of rail movement for too much of the collection and delivery of small freight consignments. The main system must be cleared for a greater volume of profitable, long distance, bulk travel.

The writing was certainly on the wall for many branch lines and country stations.

On 30 October, in a speech to the Institute of Directors, Dr Beeching was more upbeat, stating that he hoped to attract 90 million tons of freight traffic currently transported by road that was more suitable to rail. He foresaw chartered or company trains painted in the livery of the company. He also announced the introduction of 'liner trains' which would be flatbed wagons on which businesses could place their own containers. These would operate between a limited number of depots with modern handling facilities.

British Railways Workshops

On 19 September, the BTC announced that it intended to cut the workforce in their workshops from 50,000 to 38,000. The National Union of Railwaymen (NUR) reacted by announcing a one-day strike on 3 October to oppose it. In the Southern the effect would be the closure of Ashford loco works, although their wagon works would expand, with a further 150 staff being taken on. This would be at the expense of Lancing, which would be run down over the following three years with a total of 1,670 jobs being lost.

At Eastleigh, the loco works would lose 850 jobs before 1967, with only 400 jobs remaining. The carriage works that employed 1,450 people would lose its entire wagon works to Ashford, but container work would stay, meaning that 420 jobs were safe.

Channel Tunnel

At a speech by BTC member Mr L. H. Williams at a conference in Harrogate, he spoke in favour of a Channel Tunnel. He estimated that construction would take five years at a cost of £130 million. He went on to say that a new freight line would be built from Dover, avoiding London, to link with the Midlands and the North. He stated that in 1960, 55 per cent of Germany's heavy freight was moved by rail compared to only 41 per cent at home.

Ferries

The Isle of Wight ferry between Portsmouth and Fishbourne received two new ferries, *Fishbourne* and *Camber Queen*. These replaced three older ferries and brought sailing times down from one hour to 35 minutes. The ships had ramps at either end to allow easier access for vehicles and could carry thirty-four cars and 165 passengers.

Accidents

Barnham was the scene of a derailment on 3 August. The 10:17 Brighton–Portsmouth Harbour was approaching the station at 11:03 when it was derailed by a partially open facing point, forcing the leading coach towards the station ramp and overturning it. The Civil Defence and WVS helped the emergency services rescue the thirty-seven passengers who were injured – none seriously. Investigation showed that a loose washer had been the cause of the accident. This washer had been dropped by an electrical engineer and had bridged the gap between the reverse operating wire and the frame of the controller, causing the points to move. It could not be ascertained when, and therefore who, had dropped the washer. The line was open again early the following day.

At Tonbridge on 2 August, three wagons became derailed while being shunted across the main lines by No. D2179. This blocked the Down line and fouled the points on the Up line, causing considerable chaos.

On 29 October, an unattended four-car electric train ran away from Bromley North and rolled 1½ miles before crashing into a bridge abutment at Grove Park station.

Closures

The Upwey goods branch was closed on 1 January, although a number of wagons were still parked and needed to be cleared. Passenger services had been withdrawn in 1952.

The Botley–Bishop's Waltham freight branch closed on 30 April. It had lost its passenger services as long ago as 1932.

The Meon Valley line that ran from Alton to Fareham had lost its passenger services in 1955 but it closed completely on 30 April, although a train was run on 9 May to clear any remaining wagons. The line was used for a short while to store open wagons.

At the start of the year the Minister of Transport reported that talks had been held regarding the closure of all the remaining lines on the Isle of Wight. He gave an assurance that any closure would not take place in the following nine years. By August this date had been brought forward to 1967.

New Locos

The first of six experimental electro-diesels, No. E6001, started trials on 5 February, making round trips from Eastleigh to Basingstoke with empty coaching stock. They were capable of operating from the third rail or from diesel engines and were able to switch from one to another without stopping. They were built by the English Electric Co. at their Newton-le-Willows workshops. They were designed so they could operate in multiple with other electro-diesels, diesel-electrics or other multiple units and be operated remotely from other cabs. When working under diesel power, the 1,550 hp engine was capable of hauling 700 tons of freight or a ten-coach passenger train up an incline of 1 in 70.

No. D6597, the last of the Birmingham Railway, Carriage & Wagon Company's (BRCW) Type 3 diesels, was delivered to Hither Green in May.

The first of nineteen 'East Sussex' or 'Oxted' three-car DEMUs, No. 1301, was delivered in April and used for crew training at Tunbridge Wells West. No. 1302 was used on trial runs from Eastleigh to Basingstoke and No. 1303 from Eastleigh to Romsey. Both of these were transferred to St Leonards on 3 May. On 7 June a fifteen-coach train made up of Nos 1301/4/5/8/9 left Eastleigh to go to Lancing. They were built to operate services between Victoria and East Grinstead, Tunbridge Wells and Brighton via Eridge. Many of these Eastleigh-built units were late being delivered as there had been mass resignations from Eastleigh Works following the Transport Secretary Ernest Marples' announcement that the works would close in 1963.

The writing was on the wall for the USA 0-6-0Ts working the 80 miles of track at Southampton Docks. The first one was replaced by No. D2986 at Southampton on 21 June. This was one of fourteen (Nos D2985–D2998) 0-6-0 shunters built by Ruston & Hornsby. At the time there was a campaign to keep heavy loads off the roads but the shunters were delivered to the Docks on the back of a Pickfords low-loader!

Shed Closures

Ashford (73F) shed closed in June. By the time the end of this once busy shed came, it was home to a single H Class, No. 31263, a handful of C Class 0-6-0s and some BR 2-6-4Ts.

Bricklayers Arms (73B) closed in the same month. This was home to a solitary C Class, No. 31510, five N Class Moguls, four BB/WCs and three BR 2-6-4Ts.

Loco Movements

A stranger to the region in the shape of ex-GWR 4-4-0 No. 9017 travelled light from Old Oak Common to Brighton, where it was turned before it made its way to the Bluebell Railway.

LMR engines were often seen working oil trains from Fawley Refinery. Apart from Black 5s, Royal Scots and Jubilees were spotted, including No. 46122 *The Royal Ulster Rifleman*, No. 46141 *The North Staffordshire Regiment*, No. 45682 *Trafalgar* and No. 45685 *Barfleur*.

A tour of London and the Home Counties by the Electric Traction Society was planned for 16 September, hauled by a 2,500 hp electric loco. It was a comprehensive tour of the Southern suburban area for the princely sum of £1.

No. D6503 was loaned from Hither Green depot and ventured into deepest Hampshire to work the oil trains from Fawley to see if double-heading the heavier trains could be avoided by using diesels, but they also needed assistance from steam locos, with No. 82012 being used on at least one occasion. By the end of June, diesels were regularly used on boat trains from Southampton. Eastleigh had an allocation of twelve D65XX locos, but all maintenance was still carried out at Hither Green.

Last of Classes

1962 was a bad year for trainspotters, with the last examples of classes 0298, 700, C2X, E6, G16, H16, K, L, LN, N15, Schools and Z all disappearing.

Miscellanea

The year started badly, with deep snow causing major disruption to many lines.

At Weymouth on the tramway, the line was raised where it dipped under the Town Bridge. This was because it was prone to flooding during spring tides, which led to delays of up to two hours.

On 29 April the new signal box at Ashford opened, completing the colour-light signalling programme in Kent.

The Pines Express was diverted from the Somerset and Dorset line at the start of the winter services, its new route being via Basingstoke and Oxford. The last trip over the Somerset & Dorset Joint Railway (SDJR) was on 8 September and was hauled by No. 92220 *Evening Star*.

Immigrant boats were arriving at Southampton Docks and the D65XX diesels were used to take the newcomers forward to Waterloo.

Shoreham was becoming unlucky for West Countries to fail at and set fire to the track. On 26 June, No. 34013 *Okehampton* dropped a plug while working the Brighton–Plymouth service. This required the fire to be thrown out, resulting in the track catching fire. The local fire brigade had to be called to put the flames out. No. 30923 *Bradfield* eventually arrived to take over the running. The return working had caught fire there in 1961.

The winter timetable saw many cuts in services for economic reasons. These included the end of the Eastbourne–Wolverhampton and Brighton–Bournemouth services as well as reductions in frequencies between Brighton–Worthing and on the Cuckoo Line through Heathfield.

A Bill went before Parliament increasing the fine for non-payment of fares from £2 to £25. The penalty was also to be increased from one month's imprisonment to three months for altering the date on your ticket or printing your own!

At the end of the year, Southern locomotive stock consisted of 386 steam, 113 diesel-electric shunters, forty-one diesel mechanical shunters, ninety-eight diesel-electric, six electro-diesels and twenty-seven electric locos.

There were also seventy-five DEMUs working on the Southern. These consisted of twenty-three six-car units for the Hastings–Charing Cross service, four two-car units for the Hastings–Ashford line, nineteen three-car Oxted units and twenty-nine three-car Hampshire units. Typically these could run for between ten and fourteen days between servicing, by which time the brake linings would need to be replaced.

Experimental yellow warning panels were applied to the ends of multiple units and an inverted black triangle was introduced to replace the orange 'V' introduced previously. The 'V' stayed on a few units until 1965, when they had all been repainted.

A brace of E2s at Southampton Docks. No. 32101 stands in front of No. 32106 with extended side tanks in February 1962.

Another E2 at Southampton Docks on the same day was No. 32104. It was one of the last two survivors of the class, being withdrawn in April 1963.

Staying in Southampton Docks and with an E2 in the background was USA 0-6-0T No. 30063.

Ideal for shunting on docksides with sharp radius points were the diminutive 0-4-0T B4s. No. 30102 was also at Southampton Docks in February 1962.

A trip to the Isle of Wight in February and O2 0-4-4T 24 *Calbourne* was in good external condition when seen at Ryde.

On shed at Ryde on the same day was No. 30 *Shorwell* waiting for its next turn.

A tram is about to set off along Ryde Pier as a train arrives at Ryde Esplanade in February 1962.

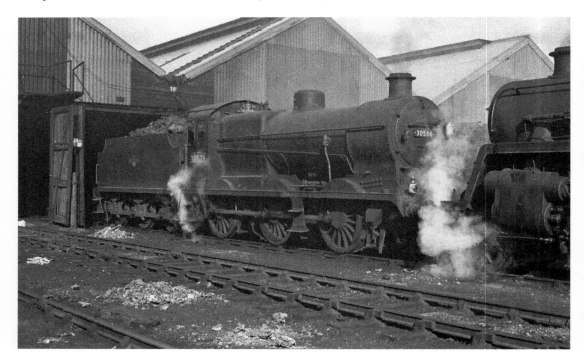

On the same day as the previous photograph and still in steam at Eastleigh was Q class 0-6-0 No. 30536.

No. 30582 was a Class 0415 and looking in remarkably good condition despite having been withdrawn for a year when this photograph was taken. This engine and two others survived about twenty years longer than the rest of the class as they were the only class of engine capable of working the tight bends and gradients of the Lyme Regis branch.

N15 No. 30770, devoid of its nameplate *Sir Prianius*, stands in front of a row of coal wagons at Eastleigh in March 1962. It had another seven months to work before being withdrawn.

Another King Arthur, which was withdrawn within four weeks of this photograph being taken in February 1962, was No. 30773 *Sir Lavaine*.

H Class No. 31005 was still working for its living in June 1962, and is seen here near Ashurst on the Kent/Sussex border.

A dog seems to be taking more interest than its owners as U1 No. 31909 passes through Ashurst on 12 June 1962.

Unrebuilt West Country No. 34002 *Salisbury* was at Southampton Docks in February 1962.

Q1 No. 33008 reverses empty stock out of Basingstoke. (Courtesy Ben Brooksbank)

Class E4 0-6-2T No. 32557 on the turntable at Nine Elms shed on 12 August 1962.

A1X No. 32640 runs round its two-coach train at Hayling Island in February 1962.

A wintry scene at Hove as a 2-BIL arrives on 30 December 1962. (Courtesy Edwin Wilmshurst)

No. 30518, an
H16 4-6-2T, was
photographed at its
home shed of Feltham
during 1962.

A new Class 207
DMU No. 1306 leaves
Riddlesdown Tunnel,
near Croydon, in
the summer of 1962.
(Courtesy Keith
Harwood)

A WR 2-6-2 Prairie
tank No. 6161
found its way onto
Southern metals at
Basingstoke having
made its way from
Reading. (Courtesy
Ben Brooksbank)

Two views of 2-BIL unit No. 2088 after having derailed and overturned at Barnham station on 3 August. Passengers appear to be wandering all over the crash scene. (Courtesy Ian Nolan)

Chapter 4

1963

1 January

On 1 January the British Railways Board (BRB) took over from the BTC with Dr Beeching as its Chairman. The new Board also took over the Road Motor Division, which was responsible for 15,000 lorries and tractors.

Also on 1 January, the Pullman Car Co. merged with British Railways and British Transport Hotels. Although until then the company had been a separate business, its shares were totally owned by the BTC. This was leading to staffing problems with unions, so fully integrating with BR was seen as the answer.

On 20 March, staff at the Pullman Car Works at Preston Park were told that the works would close early in 1964. After closure, SR Pullmans would be maintained at Eastleigh and ER ones at York. Just prior to becoming part of BR, the staff had been told their jobs were safe for at least two or three years.

On the same date, all lines west of Salisbury came under the control of the Western Region. This meant the transfer of 149 locomotives and the transfer of sheds at Exmouth Junction (72A), Yeovil (72C), Barnstaple Junction (72E) and Wadebridge (72F). Salisbury shed code was changed from 72B to 70E.

The Reshaping of British Railways Report

More commonly referred to as the Beeching Report, 'The Reshaping of British Railways Report' was published on 27 March. It was broadly accepted by the government, with reservations that it could subsidise some lines that they may wish to keep open although they were not commercially viable.

The report recommended that 2,300 stations close, as well as 800 freight-handling depots. Passenger services on 266 lines nationwide were threatened with closure, with a further seventy-one being modified. Lines on the Southern that were recommended for closure included Guildford–Christ's Hospital–Shoreham, Guildford–Reigate, Redhill–Tonbridge, Tunbridge Wells–Three Bridges, Eridge–Polegate, Crowborough–Lewes, the Somerset & Dorset, Brockenhurst–Bournemouth via Ringwood and the Mid-Hants line.

The Unions distributed a leaflet urging the public to oppose the closures and instructing them on how to do so. The leaflet stated that any proposed branch or station closure had to be advertised by posters on stations at least six weeks before the proposed closure date and an advert placed in two local newspapers for two consecutive weeks. Any objections should be based on hardship caused, citing that the proposed bus service would take far longer and be less frequent, making the working day unreasonably long, would cost more, and that they could not cater for prams, bicycles or parcels. All objections had to be considered by the BRB and if no objections were submitted the closure would happen without any further delay.

Ryde Pier, Isle of Wight

On 29 September, Ryde Pier closed to rail services for major repairs. The pier was built in 1880 and had had no major works done on it since. A recent survey showed that it needed major renovations and it was thought that it might have to close entirely. A decision was taken, however, to carry out the repairs needed at a cost of £250,000. This money was to be spent on completely renewing the decking on the existing iron piers, which were still in good condition. Although the Beeching Report had been published, it was thought that the island's railway services would be spared as they had been given assurances from the British Transport Commission that five years' notice of closure would be given for the Ryde–Cowes line and seven years for the Ryde–Ventnor line. Closure of the pier led to operational difficulties as there were no run-round facilities at Ryde Esplanade. Trains from Ventnor went there but trains from Cowes stopped at Ryde St John's Road. Passengers for the mainland had to transfer to a train from Ventnor. Another engine was attached to the rear of this train and it continued to Ryde Esplanade with a loco on each end. For the return journey, the loco at the rear was detached when the train reached St John's Road and passengers for Cowes had to change. The tramway continued to run on a separate pier and this was used to ferry passengers to the Pier Head. The works were completed in April 1964 and normal service resumed.

New Techniques

The workshops at Eastleigh had been experimenting with using different types of materials and during 1963 produced the first coach body made from plastic. It had been built onto the chassis of one of the coaches crushed by a falling bridge in the 1957 Lewisham disaster. Advantages in using plastic were that the colour was added to the resin, meaning it did not need painting and it was not subject to rust. The coach did not have the traditional framework, but strength was created by using a construction of rigid polyurethane foam sandwiched between an inner and outer skin of glass resin. The coach was used on the *Lancing Belle* and then on the Hayling Island branch line for a while before returning to the *Lancing Belle*. It was originally numbered DS70200. While working at Hayling Island it was renumbered S1000S but returned to its original number when resuming 'Belle' duties. The coach survives at the East Somerset Railway. A second coach was built for crash-testing purposes. It was not just whole coaches that benefited from new techniques – the cab roofs of the E6XXX locos were also made this way, as well as plastic doors being fitted to metal coaches. These doors stood up to rigorous testing in the workshops better than doors made using traditional methods.

Accidents

On 8 February at 08:46 at Drayton, the 07:50 Portsmouth Harbour–Brighton ran into the back of the 07:37 Portsmouth Harbour–Bognor Regis in thick fog. The earlier train had been stopped at a signal and was slowly accelerating away when it was hit.

Seventeen of the 210 passengers were injured, though none seriously, as were the driver and guard of the Brighton train. The Chichester branch of the WVS helped the emergency services and all the injured were on their way to hospital by 09:20.

Damage was mainly confined to the rear two coaches of the Bognor train and the cab of the Brighton train, with both being completely wrecked and both motor bogies suffering serious damage.

Blame was put partly on the guard of the first train for being too slow in informing the signalman that his train had stopped at a signal in thick fog. Two signalmen were also partly blamed for miscommunication, which is why the second train was allowed into the section. The driver of the Brighton train did not escape criticism either, as when he had seen the train in front he had relied on releasing the dead man's handle to stop his train, without realising there was a 5-second delay. He should have applied the brakes himself.

On 10 September, at 13:47, the 11:20 Dover Marine–Hither Green train of ferry vans became derailed on a section of curved track between Longfield and Farningham Road while travelling at about 60 mph. Eighteen vans were derailed and they travelled 185 yards, badly damaging the track before they came to a halt. The train parted between the first and second vans but the automatic braking system failed to work and locomotive No. E5008 travelled over a mile before stopping. The report into the accident said there was no apparent cause of the derailment, but speed limits of 50 mph were subsequently applied.

On 20 November the 11:47 Salisbury–Chichester freight was wrongly routed into Platform 4 at Eastleigh, where it collided with three-car DEMU No. 1103. Luckily no one was injured but No. 30838, in charge of the freight, suffered front end damage.

Accidents were not confined to BR's network and on 3 June the Romney, Hythe & Dymchurch suffered a rare accident. 4-8-2 *Hercules* failed near Hythe while working a packed fourteen-coach train. The relief train behind, 4-6-2 *Typhoon*, ran into the back of it while travelling at speed. The last carriages of the first train and five coaches on the relief train were all derailed. The accident could have been much worse as another train hauled by *Winston Churchill* was passing in the opposite direction at the time but did not make contact with any of the derailed coaches. Around twenty passengers sustained injuries but thankfully there were no fatalities. 4-6-2 *Green Goddess* was dispatched tender first to bring back the coaches of the relief train that had not derailed. Another 4-6-2, *Northern Chief*, was then sent to the scene with a breakdown crane. After the damaged coaches had been re-railed and taken away by *Hercules*, three locos – *Green Goddess*, *Winston Churchill* and *Northern Chief* – brought back the remaining coaches and breakdown train, all coupled together to form one thirty-six-vehicle train.

New Stock

The last of the 4-CEPs (Nos 7205–11), were delivered to work services on the Western Division from Waterloo.

An order was placed for the first of 138 four-car electric units to replace the old stock on the Brighton line (Nos 7301–7438). These were categorised as 4-CIG (Corridor Intermediate Guards) and were to be built at BR's workshops at York and introduced from 1964–70. There were also eighteen 4-BIG (Buffet Intermediate Guards) introduced in 1965–6 (Nos 7031–48), with a further ten in 1970 (Nos 7049–58). They were to replace the 6-PUL and 6-PAN units that were over thirty years old and had clocked up over 3 million miles each.

Loco Movements

Southampton Football Club made it to the FA Cup Semi-Finals and their opponents were Manchester United. The match was played at Aston Villa's ground in Birmingham. On the morning of the match, fourteen steam specials left Southampton between 07:00 and 09:00. These travelled via Basingstoke and Reading West. Another train left Brockenhurst and was routed via Bournemouth and the S&D. West Country's were in charge of most of the specials and sheds including Nine Elms, Eastleigh, Bournemouth and Salisbury were responsible for supplying the motive power.

Easter needed a number of reliefs to satisfy demand and on the Thursday before Good Friday, the 18:00 from Waterloo to the West of England needed two reliefs, with No. 34052, No. 35025 and No. 34060 being in charge. The 18:30 to Bournemouth and Weymouth needed three reliefs and Nos 34064, 34014, 35008 and 73119 were in charge of the four trains.

Training trips for Type 3 diesels were run from New Cross Gate to Polegate during the end of April. They were also making their presence felt on the south coast, taking over from several steam turns including the 09:40 Brighton to Bournemouth and the 13:45 return journey.

The last M7 to work the Seaton branch, No. 30048, made the journey on 2 May with the 11:40 from Seaton. Bunting in the station's goods yard marked the event. The service continued but in the hands of GWR 0-6-0 pannier tanks.

Last of Classes

The following classes all disappeared from the network: A1X, B4, E2, E4, T9 and U1. Billy Butlin was reported as wishing to buy five A1Xs, but he was told there was a waiting list from preservation societies to buy them.

Lines Closed

The tramway on the West Quay at Newhaven Harbour closed on 10 August when Terrier No. 32678 cleared the remaining wagons. This was partly because a factory on the quay that produced ropes and tarpaulins ceased production. A1Xs were the only locos allowed over the swing bridge to the West Quay and as this closed, Newhaven shed was not needed, and it closed on 9 September.

The Hayling Island branch also closed on Saturday 2 November. A summer service operated on this last day with one express and one stopping train per hour in each direction. The three-coach trains were very well patronised, with Nos 32650/62/70 in charge. No. 32662 carried a wreath on its smokebox door. Hayling Island Preservation Society was formed hoping to acquire the line and run it as an electric tramway with stock from the GCML line from Grimsby.

Another line to lose its service was Haywards Heath–Horsted Keynes, which closed on 27 October with the last scheduled passenger train being a 6-PAN unit, No. 3033, working the 18:16 Horsted Keynes–Seaford. This was closely followed by an excursion headed by A1X *Stepney* and E4 *Birch Grove* that returned later in the evening.

Sheds Closed

Basingstoke (70D) closed in March. At that time it was home to one Q, No. 30541, three U Class Moguls, and six BR Class 4 4-6-0s.

St Leonards (74E) closed to steam in July, although it had not had its own allocation since 1958.

Stewarts Lane closed in September. Its last days of operation saw a few Maunsell 2-6-0s still allocated there but they were outnumbered by various Standard (Std) types.

Tunbridge Wells West closed in September. Apart from Std Class 4 tanks, there were still a handful of Class H and M7s 0-4-4Ts.

Ashford (73F) closed in June. It had been home to the remaining Cs and a lone H, No. 31263.

Miscellanea

Cannon Street station was rebuilt, with the old station hotel being demolished and a new office block erected in its place.

Local press reported that the Bournemouth line was going to be electrified using overhead wires, utilising six-car sets with an electric loco at either end.

The large exhibits section of the Railway Museum at Clapham opened and included five royal saloons as well as static steam engines.

A late Brighton Belle was introduced for the winter timetable to serve theatre-goers making their way home to the south coast. It left at 23:00 but starting serving food from 22:00 while standing at Victoria station.

The Oxted lines saw their last scheduled steam passenger service on Sunday 7 September, with the last trip being the 17:06 Tunbridge Wells–London Bridge in the hands of BR 2-6-4T No. 80142. Dieselisation caused a problem as the majority of coaching stock on the lines was steam-heated and with winter approaching, stock had to be found with electric heating apparatus and coaches were brought in from other regions and maroon stock could be seen with their numbers given an 'S' prefix.

From August, any Std Class 5s going through Eastleigh Works were repainted in lined green livery.

An electric loco was booked to operate a Royal Train for the first time when it took the President of Iceland from Gatwick to Victoria, but it disgraced itself by breaking down on the way to the airport. No. D6529 was substituted to work the train made up of three Pullmans.

A new service from Fawley oil refinery to Bromford Bridge, Birmingham, was initiated on 3 December. It was publicised in the national press and on television. The inaugural service saw double-headed Class 3 diesels hauling fifty-four tankers measuring 450 yards.

A delivery of poor coal led to six failures on the Reading–Redhill line on 3 December, with Nos 31400, 31633, 31797, 31806/17/62 all succumbing and an evening freight service having to be cancelled due to lack of motive power.

No. 32479 had a second lease of life, as although it had been in store at Hove awaiting disposal, it was put back into traffic early in 1963 for shunting duties at Newhaven, where it deputised for a diesel shunter. Its last day of work was 19 May. It was finally withdrawn from Brighton in June and was scrapped at Eastleigh in July.

No. 30368 was a Class 700 0-6-0 introduced in 1897 by Drummond. It was photographed in 1963 after being withdrawn at the end of 1962. It was cut up in December '63.

This was the scene at Hove dump in 1963 with K Class No. 32338 at the head of a line of condemned locos.

Another engine at Hove dump in 1963 was E4 No. 32468, an R. Billinton design of 1910.

Another E4 waiting for the cutter's torch was No. 32557 at Eastleigh.

Battle of Britain Class No. 34086 *219 Squadron* at Exeter St Davids on 23 May, working the Plymouth–Brighton service.

BIL No. 2084 at Ardingly on a Horsted Keynes–Seaford stopping service on 30 March. (Courtesy Ian Nolan)

BR STD 4MT 2-6-0 No. 76011 waits to leave Salisbury for Bournemouth West. (Courtesy Ben Brooksbank)

On 1 June, ex-LMS 2-6-2T No. 41312 was on shed at Brighton. (Courtesy Charlie Verrall)

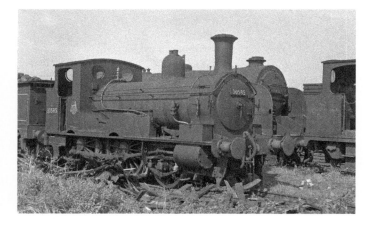

No. 30585 was one of three 2-4-0 Beattie well tanks that had worked on the Bodmin & Wadebridge Railway since 1895. It was photographed at Eastleigh after the branch closed in December 1962. It escaped the cutter's torch and was purchased by the Quainton Road Railway Society.

The Hayling Island Farewell Tour took place on 3 November 1963. The tour started from London Waterloo behind S15 No. 30512. At Havant, No. 32636 took over for the trip over the Langstone Viaduct.

No. 32670 had been on the rear of the train on its trip to the island, so was in position to pull the train back to Havant, where a pair of Qs, Nos 30531 and 30543, took the enthusiasts back to London.

No. 20002 was spotted at Three Bridges during 1963. It was a Bulleid design introduced in 1941. It was capable of running off the third rail or by overhead wires. It later had a headcode panel fitted. It was withdrawn in December 1968.

No. 30503 was a Urie-designed S15 introduced in March 1921. It served for forty-two years before being withdrawn from Feltham shed in July 1963.

Chapter 5

1964

Electrification to Bournemouth

In September, the Minister of Transport authorised the commencement of the extension of the third rail network to Bournemouth. This consisted of 236 track miles over 90 route miles and would cost £15 million.

Trains from Waterloo would be twelve-car formations made up of three four-car units with only one unit being powered. This would be a 3,200 hp 4-REP (Restaurant Electro Pneumatic) unit marshalled at the London end of the train. A total of 128 carriages would be needed, of which ninety-five would be unpowered. Many of these trailer units would be converted from loco-hauled stock.

The line from Bournemouth to Weymouth was not included in the electrification scheme so some Class 33 diesels had to be converted to push-pull operation to work the new stock from Bournemouth. The four or eight coaches nearest Weymouth would be uncoupled and the Class 33 attached for the onward journey. Similarly, on the return journey, the push-pull train would be coupled up to the coaches waiting at Bournemouth and the Class 33 detached.

The new scheme would start at Pirbright Junction through Bournemouth to Branksome, where new maintenance sheds would be built on the site of the old Bournemouth West station. The Durnsford Road depot at Wimbledon would also be modernised to maintain the electric stock. Eastleigh would be responsible for maintaining the diesels and electro-diesels. Weymouth would be provided with a refuelling point.

Southampton boat trains would continue to be locomotive-hauled using diesels or electro-diesels. A number of Class 33 diesels would be transferred from the Central and South Eastern Divisions and these would be replaced by electro-diesels.

Prior to electrification being completed, the line from Waterloo to Bournemouth was the last 100 per cent steam-hauled express service in the country. The electrification scheme would spell the end for the Bournemouth Belle.

4-CIG Units

The first of 138 4-CIGs were delivered to Selhurst. They were built at York for the Western and Central Divisions. The first batch were numbered 7301–36, bore green livery, and were for use on the Brighton lines. The first new unit, No. 7301, was on display at Waterloo on 6 November. It had made a test run to Brighton on 14 October, followed by further return trips to Ford.

They were corridor throughout, differing from previous electric units by having the motor coach in a middle coach and driver trailer units at either end. Second-class accommodation was all in open-plan seating, except for one compartment, which was next to three first-class compartments in one of the driving trailers.

Last Atlantic Coast Express

On Friday 4 September, the last steam-hauled Atlantic Coast Express (ACE) left Waterloo at 11:00 behind gleaming Merchant Navy Class No. 35022 *Holland-America Line*, hauling a load of thirteen coaches packed with enthusiasts. The Up train on the same day had been in the hands of a diesel-hydraulic Warship Class loco, as it had been since 17 August and as would future Down trains. Apart from a signal check at Nine Elms, progress was good, and the train arrived at Salisbury 2 minutes early. The engine took on water there and the crews changed before departing again for Exeter Central, where it arrived 1 minute late. The train split here, with the front portion going to Ilfracombe while No. 34015 *Exmouth* was attached to the rear portion that carried on to Padstow.

Lancing Belle

This ran for the last time on 3 July. It had been steam-hauled until 15 June, when a Type 3 diesel took over. The diesel was not allowed into the works so the train was met at the gates by a USA 0-6-0T, which took the carriages through the works to the platform at the western end. The train continued to run using electric stock. It did not enter the works but terminated at Lancing station.

Accidents

Two goods trains collided at Itchingfield at 03:00 on 5 March. Itchingfield was the junction where the line from Brighton via Steyning met the Mid-Sussex line from Pulborough to Horsham. One of the trains was the 02:00 Brighton–Three Bridges unfitted freight that had been diverted via Steyning due to engineering works. It consisted of thirty-four wagons hauled by a Class 33 diesel, No. D6502. This train ran through a red signal and collided with a fifty-four-wagon freight train coming in the opposite direction. This train had also been diverted due to engineering works and was diesel-hauled. The driver of this train saw the impending accident and applied his brakes. The Up goods struck the nineteenth wagon of the Down train, hitting it and the wagon behind it at a glancing angle. It continued on, demolishing wagons in its path until it reached the thirtieth wagon, which was much heavier, being a 50-ton bogie wagon loaded with wheels and axles. The impact destroyed the diesel's cab and overturned it, killing both crew members. Emergency services were soon on the scene but the damage was so extensive that the bodies of the crew could not be extricated from the wreckage until around noon that day. It had been the third consecutive night that the Up crew had worked the same duty and the two previous nights had passed the junction without delay.

The inquiry found that the driver had to bear the brunt of the responsibility for the accident as he had passed a signal at danger, but his second man had to bear some responsibility as it was also his duty to keep an eye on signals. It was assumed that both crew members may have nodded off in the hot, stuffy atmosphere in the cab due to the heaters, and some heat being dissipated from the engine, although there was no evidence of toxic fumes from the engine. Three breakdown cranes were used to clear the wreckage and both running lines were open the following day. No. D6502 was written off and had to be cut up at the scene two months later.

USA tank No. 30068 had been working at Betteshanger Colliery but sustained damage in an accident there and had to return to Ashford for repairs.

On 1 January, the SS *St Patrick* hit the quay wall at Southampton after arriving from Le Havre, damaging her bow. There were no dry docks available at Southampton so she was taken to Cardiff for repairs. The service was suspended for three weeks. Passengers for Paris were advised to go via Victoria or travel by the cargo ship *Haselmere*, which sailed once every week and could accommodate twelve passengers. The ferry route was due to close and was awaiting the Minister's approval after an inquiry had been held by the Transport Users' Consultative Committee (TUCC). It ended on 9 May when the SS *St Patrick* arrived. She continued to sail from Southampton but now to St Malo.

Line Closures

The Deptford Wharf branch closed on 1 January. Coal traffic on the line had been dwindling for some time, although the main reason for its closure was the failure of the Hatcham lifting bridge during 1963. A breakdown crane had been stabled nearby to raise the bridge should any vessel using the Surrey Canal wish to pass.

Notices were posted on the Isle of Wight stating that all train services would end on 12 October unless objections were received. They were!

The Ringwood branch closed on 2 May with No. 82028 in charge of the last trip, the 19:08 Bournemouth West–Brockenhurst, and the 20:56 return journey.

The Fordingbridge line closed to passenger traffic on the same day with the last train being the 8:30 p.m. from Salisbury, a nine-coach train headed by No. 76066 carrying a wreath on the smokebox door. Detonators were set off and crowds cheered as it left. It was greeted at Fordingbridge by packed platforms, the local Carnival Queen and a band playing 'The Last Post'. Daggons Road had a fireworks display and it was held up there as someone took the tail lamp as a memento. However, when it reached its destination – Bournemouth Central – there was no one there to greet it!

Through goods services on the Didcot, Newbury and Southampton line closed on 10 August. All freight trains were subsequently re-routed via Basingstoke and Reading. Passenger services had been withdrawn on 7 March 1960 with T9 No. 30120 hauling the last Down train.

The Romsey–Andover line closed on 7 September. The last Up train was worked by DEMU No. 1127. Many locals took the opportunity for one last journey. At Andover the train was met by civic dignitaries and a band playing 'The Last Post'. Unit No. 1105 was in charge of the last Down train.

The Midhurst–Pulborough line was officially closed on 16 October. The *Midhurst Belle* was run on 18 October, with Q No. 30530 being the first steam engine over the line for quite a while. Freight continued as far as Petworth until May 1966.

The Bexhill West branch closed on 15 June. The last train left Bexhill West for Crowhurst at 22:20. It was packed with enthusiasts including two passengers who had also been on the first train in 1902.

Last of Classes

Classes M7, W and H all disappeared from the system. The M7s had once been used on empty stock workings from Waterloo, but had been replaced by Std Class 3 2-6-2Ts. The start of 1964 saw any survivors of the class in pretty awful condition and those based at Horsham were moved westwards to bolster numbers there. Hampshire DEMUs were taking over some of their workings and they were finally confined to working the Swanage and Lymington branches. These were the last push-pull workings on the Southern.

A class of diesels became extinct with the withdrawal of No. 15202, one of six shunters introduced in 1948.

Sheds Closed

Faversham (73E) and Three Bridges (75E) both closed on 5 January. Norwood closed to steam on 6 January, although diesels continued to be stabled there. Reading South, a sub shed to Guildford, closed on 6 April. Horsham (75E) closed on 15 June with Three Bridges supplying any engines still needed. Brighton shed also closed to steam on the same date but continued to stable diesels, although it was envisaged that these would be moved to Lovers Walk electric depot. Any locomotives that needed servicing were sent to Eastbourne.

Loco Movements

A Jubilee, No. 45672 *Anson*, that had failed at Newhaven and No. 45617 *Mauritius* arrived at Eastbourne when someone had noticed that Jubilees were not allowed over the Central Division and were impounded. Another unusual visitor to the shed at the same time was B1 No. 61313 that had worked a pigeon special from Canklow to Lewes and suffered from a hot box. These were joined by Nos 44862 and 73159, making a rare sight at Eastbourne shed. No. 61313 found its way to Redhill, where it was kept for a while working empty coaching stock to Brighton and passenger services to and from Reading before working a freight to Cricklewood as the first leg of its journey home.

There had been a build-up of locomotives at sheds awaiting scrapping so some were sent to private yards for disposal. Locos made the journey from Feltham to Kettering as a Class 8 freight train. These included Qs, Q1s and Ws. Three Schools were also sent from Nine Elms and a number of Moguls went from Stewarts Lane to Norwich. Stewarts Lane was clear of condemned engines after the last two locos, Nos 31305 and 31542, were taken away to Briton Ferry, South Wales, for scrapping.

Miscellanea

B4 No. 30096 was purchased by Corralls Ltd and started work at Dibbles Wharf in Southampton, where it replaced a Peckett 0-4-0ST Bristol. Sister engine No. 30102 was taken by road from Redbridge to Butlins at Ayr after being restored to LSWR livery at Eastleigh.

At the start of the year many engines were arriving at Eastleigh for scrap, with several arriving under their own steam including No. 30700 towing No. 30832, and No. 30931 towing No. 30689. No. 30053 towed No. 31543 from Three Bridges and then carried on to Bournemouth.

On 4/5 January, the last through steam workings from Brighton took place with No. 34070 on the Plymouth train and No. 34072 on the Bournemouth service. Subsequent workings were in the hands of 20001 Class electric locomotives.

The only steam workings left from Brighton were those to Horsham, which were all in the hands of Ivatt 2-6-2Ts.

A Hymek, No. D7008, appeared at Waterloo on 28 January for the first time. It brought the empty stock of the Oxford–Brentford football excursion into the terminus to be cleaned and serviced after football hooligans had trashed it.

Other Western Region motive power was used over Southern rails when Manors were used on the Reading–Redhill service. No. 7829 *Ramsbury Manor* was one such locomotive used on 7 August.

The first of the 6-PUL units was withdrawn from service in January. The Pullman cars were used on 4-RES units in place of their restaurant cars. The rest of the coaches, along with some 6-PAN units, were sent to Micheldever for disposal.

3 January saw the last steam workings at Uckfield, with Nos 31408, 80149, 80138 and 80089 all appearing during the day. The Oxted line lost its H Class push-pull sets the following day. DEMUs carried on running from then on.

From 28 March, a Regency Belle was run from Victoria to Brighton on Saturday and Sunday evenings leaving at 19:15. Passengers could sample Brighton's nightlife before catching the return train home at 02:15. On most occasions a 5-BEL unit was used, leaving Victoria from Platform 1, but during April, Battle of Britain Class No. 34088 *213 Squadron*, pulling seven Pullmans and two vans, was used. This was because on its return journey engineers had taken possession of the main line so it was diverted via Steyning which was not electrified. The service was not proving successful and on one weekend, 25/26 April, it was cancelled at short notice. For the summer service it was re-timed to leave Victoria at 21:25 in a bid to increase patronage.

Many of the through services were scrapped, including the Saturday Cardiff–Brighton, Birmingham–Hastings via Reading and the Sheffield–Hastings services. Only three inter-regional trains survived. These were the Manchester, Walsall and Wolverhampton trains all terminating at Eastbourne. The thrice-weekly Glasgow–Eastbourne car sleeper had been diverted to Newhaven, as had the once-weekly Newcastle–Dover train.

No. 30928 *Stowe* was bought by Lord Montague and was delivered by road to the National Motor Museum at Beaulieu on 14 February. While there, one of its nameplates was reported stolen. Lord Montague also purchased three Pullmans – *Fingall*, *Agatha* and *Car No. 31*. *Stowe* stayed there until 1973, when it went to the East Somerset Railway and then to the Bluebell Railway, where it was restored.

The Pullman car works at Preston Park closed in January. It was to become a store for preserved locomotives by 1967.

Electric train drivers at Brighton went on strike on Sunday 23 February. Diesels and DEMUs were drafted in to keep a service running.

DEMUs Nos 1114–8 were transferred from Hampshire to work on the Steyning line. This left many services in Hampshire worked by only one unit, rather than two, which led to overcrowding during rush hours. This was not helped by the murder of a young girl on unit No. 1107: the police impounded the coach in which she was murdered at Basingstoke and held it for three months. In November this carriage was moved to Winchester, where it was used for inspection during the trial. The driving trailer of No. 1129 was also badly damaged when involved in a collision with the tender of No. 75066 near Eastleigh Diesel Depot. The situation was eased with the closure of the Andover–Romsey line in September.

Five Terriers still existed. No. 32670 made its way from Eastleigh to the KESR. Another couple of the Class, Nos 32640/78, were being restored at Eastleigh before being sold to Billy Butlin, while No. 32636 was destined for the Bluebell Railway and No. 32646, thought at one time to be going to the Hayling Island Preservation Society, was sold to the Sadler Railcar Co. at Droxford, spending three years on the former Meon Valley Line before being moved to a plinth outside the Hayling Billy public house on the island until 1979.

Officials from the Hayling Island Preservation Society were reported to have travelled to Brussels to negotiate the purchase of tramcars to use on the line. At the time it was expected that their efforts would be successful and the line would re-open.

From the summer, the 24-hour clock was used in working timetables.

On 24 April, A4 No. 60008 *Dwight D. Eisenhower* was towed to Southampton Docks by No. 35012 *United States Line*. It was loaded aboard the USS *American Planter* three days later. No. 35012 was used again to bring Dr Beeching from Waterloo, where he officially handed over the locomotive.

From 1 June drivers started to be trained on Warship diesels, initially between Salisbury and Basingstoke, ready for when steam workings to Waterloo finally succumbed to diesel power.

Diesel-hydraulic Warship Class locos commenced running Exeter–Waterloo services on 17 August, with three return trips on weekdays.

No. 20001 headed a special train of eleven coaches, including seven Pullmans from Victoria to Newhaven on 31 May in connection with the inauguration of a new ferry, the *Falaise*.

It was suggested that a possible solution to the Isle of Wight's problem following the end of steam would be to convert some Piccadilly line tube stock to diesel power and it was noted that on 16 August twelve tube train coaches were pulled by No. D6540 from Wimbledon Park depot to Micheldever, with one carrying the words 'Ryde Pier Head'.

Lingfield race day on 28 November brought heavy demands on the service, with some DEMU services being replaced with steam. Altogether, another thirty-four extra steam trains were run, needing six locos to operate them.

A number of tenders from Eastern Region V2s arrived at Eastleigh during the autumn for conversion to snowploughs. After conversion they were taken to Crewe, Banbury and Shrewsbury. Schools Class tenders were also converted. Tender-designated No. DS70229 was taken to Salisbury, No. DS70224 to Eastleigh and another, No. DS70228, to Ashford.

Yellow warning panels started to appear on the ends of some EMUs from the end of January.

It had been decided that the region was lacking in push-pull operation so with the electrification of the Bournemouth line in mind, a 6-TC set was formed using six old pre-war coaches that had been converted for the purpose. The set was used on non-electrified lines in Sussex.

The government made the decision to go ahead with the Channel Tunnel.

No. 1301 was captured leaving Eridge on the 12:45pm Eastbourne–Tunbridge Wells service on 31 October. (Courtesy Charlie Verrall)

Crompton Type 3 No. D6571 in original green livery was seen passing Chichester with a brake van in tow. (Courtesy Trevor Tupper)

Inside Lancing Works on 29 February 1964. (Courtesy Edwin Wilmshurst)

A visitor to the Southern was Western Region Hymek No. D7034, running through Lancing with the Brighton–Cardiff service on 21 June. (Courtesy Edwin Wilmshurst)

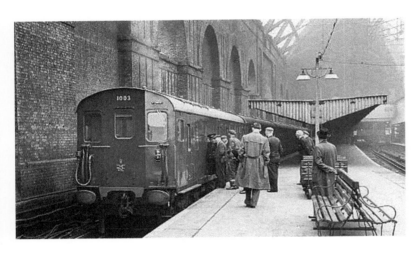

Hastings six-car unit No. 1003 waits to leave Cannon Street for Hastings.

2-BIL No. 2052 at Hampden Park heads into Eastbourne on a Brighton–Hastings service.

2-HAL No. 2634 heads through Raynes Park with a Waterloo–Alton service. (Courtesy Keith Harwood)

0-4-4T M7 No. 30133 lasted until March 1964. Its home sheds had been mainly Nine Elms and Eastleigh but it spent its last year at Salisbury.

Merchant Navy No. 35020 *Bibby Line* in superb external condition. It was withdrawn early in 1965.

Two 4-LAV units pass Coulsdon North southbound on their way to Brighton. (Courtesy Keith Harwood)

S15 No. 30843 enters Basingstoke with a freight train. It was withdrawn later on in the year (1964).

Chapter 6

1965

Cannon Street

Work had been ongoing at the terminus for some time and some improvements were now becoming evident to the public. The concourse adjacent to Platforms 1–5 was enlarged with new refreshment rooms and confectionary kiosks. Temporary left luggage and ticket offices were opened as work had commenced on the concourse adjacent to Platforms 5–8. New canopies had been erected on Platforms 1–4, with steel supports in place for canopies over other platforms. The new improvements were well received.

Clapham Junction Signal Gantry

On 10 May, the signal gantry over the tracks at Clapham Junction started to collapse. It was caused by heavy corrosion in the sixty-year-old construction. Traffic on the Windsor lines was stopped completely, but trains on the main lines were allowed to pass under the stricken box for a short while, albeit very slowly; however, even these were soon halted as it was thought that vibrations from passing trains could cause further damage, and so all trains in and out of Waterloo were halted. A 75-ton crane was sent from Nine Elms depot to support the gantry while steel trestles as used by the army were used to support it while jacks were used to raise it back to the correct level. The collapse happened during the morning rush and led to a train being held at every signal into the suburbs. Some passengers were lucky, being held at stations, while others had to be de-trained and walk along the tracks to the nearest station. By the evening rush, Wimbledon had become the terminus station for electric trains coming from Portsmouth, Guildford and the Epsom lines, while trains on the Windsor lines were turned at Barnes and Twickenham. Steam trains from Bournemouth were terminated at Woking, with the triangle at Addlestone being used to turn the locos. Boat trains were diverted to Victoria and mail and paper trains started from Victoria or Paddington. Emergency repairs were carried out to the gantry, but trestles supporting the gantry blocked access to Platforms 1 and 2. These repairs allowed most trains to run under the gantry the following day, although with much stock out of place there was still major disruption.

Later that week, temperatures of 82 degrees caused a conductor rail to buckle at Vauxhall during the evening rush hour, bringing more misery to commuters.

Winston Churchill

On 30 January, No. 34051 *Winston Churchill* was in charge of the funeral train carrying the former Prime Minister to his final resting place at Bladon in Oxfordshire, close to Blenheim Palace where he was born. It would have been more convenient to leave from Paddington, but it was his wish to use Waterloo, especially if he died before Charles de Gaulle. He had been lying in state for three days at Westminster Hall. His coffin was loaded on to a launch, *Havengore*, at Tower Pier and taken up the Thames to Waterloo Pier, where it was transferred to a motor hearse for its short trip to Waterloo station.

No. 34051's home shed was Salisbury, so it had to be sent to Nine Elms for preparation five days before the event. No. 34064 *Fighter Command* was also prepared as a stand-by engine and sent to Staines, but was not needed. The funeral train was made up of five Pullman cars and a bogie van, PMV No. S2464, which carried the coffin and was specially painted in Pullman colours for the journey. The train stopped briefly at Reading to pick up a WR pilot before continuing its journey to Hanborough. No. 34051 returned light to Nine Elms and a Class 52 diesel returned the funeral train to Paddington.

The van that carried Churchill's coffin was subsequently sold to the City of Industry, a Los Angeles municipal corporation, for £350 and was shipped to California. In 2007, an appeal to repatriate it was successful and it found a home on the Swanage Railway. It has since been fully restored and is currently at the National Railway Museum at Shildon.

4-BIG Units

Eighteen 4-BIG units were introduced in 1965/6. These were basically 4-CIG units but with a full-length buffet car instead of a trailer second coach. They were intended to make up the centre four coaches of a twelve-car train sandwiched between 4-CIG units and be used on London–Brighton and Eastbourne services. They were numbered 7031–48. Another ten units were introduced in 1970 (Nos 7049–58). After extensive trials, the first revenue-earning trip by a 4-CIG was not until 29 March, when a twelve-car train left Brighton at 08:20 for London Bridge.

Tonbridge–Reading

The Tonbridge–Redhill–Reading route was dieselised on 4 January. It had been earmarked for closure in the Beeching Report but had been spared, although the Southern posted warning notices that the decision to retain and modernise the service could only be justified if passenger usage increased. Most of the passenger journeys were in the hands of DEMUs but a few were loco-hauled. Steam was still in charge of parcel trains. There were six three-car DEMUs provided for the service. They were made up of a motor coach and trailer from a Hastings six-car set and a driving trailer from a 2-EPB unit. With this carriage being wider than the other two, they were nicknamed 'tadpole units' by the staff. They were numbered 1201–6. Although not aesthetically pleasing, they were well received by passengers, being more comfortable and cleaner than the ageing Maunsell stock they replaced. Initially failures were not uncommon and steam- and diesel-hauled trains had to substitute for the stricken DEMUs.

On the Saturday prior to the DEMUs taking over, a variety of Moguls were in charge of the service with Nos 31405/8, 31627, 31790/1/9, 31800/16/58/62 all working passenger trains. These engines were due to be dispersed after the end of this service but many had to stay in the area due to the shortage of Class 3 diesels. Some found their way to Guildford shed and were seen on parcels and freight trains to Waterloo and other South London destinations.

When the Redhill–Reading service used Reading South, cheap day tickets were available. On the closure of this station trains used Reading General. This came under the jurisdiction of the Western Region; their policy was not to issue these tickets. However, for those wishing to take advantage of Southern's offer, they could catch a bus to the Reading suburb of Earley. Another problem with using Reading General station was that the DEMUs used Platform 6, which meant crossing the GWR main lines – often leading to long delays. On Christmas and Boxing Day the Western Region closed down whereas the Southern didn't, but this meant that the Waterloo–Reading service had to terminate at Wokingham.

Accidents

On Monday 8 March, a freight train derailed at Streatham Junction. Twenty wagons came off the tracks just north of the platforms at Streatham Common, blocking all four main lines. Local trains were diverted via Mitcham Junction and Sutton, while Brighton line trains had to go via the Crystal Palace loop and Norwood Junction to East Croydon. The line remained closed for two days.

Another derailment occurred at Folkestone East on 12 February. The Down van train stopped to unload at the station with its loco No. E5006 straddling the points leading to the boat train sidings. A decision was taken to shunt the train into the sidings to clear the main line but the track circuit had been wired wrongly and the signalman received a false 'clear' signal on his illuminated console and changed the points beneath the loco. When the loco pulled forward the leading bogie followed the track for the main line and the trailing bogie headed for the sidings. The loco became derailed and the breakdown crane from Ashford was summoned. A temporary bus service between Folkestone Central and Dover Priory was implemented while the line was blocked.

On 22 August, 2-BIL No. 2105 was in collision with a Southdown bus on the Roundstone level crossing near Worthing. The accident happened in thick fog.

The train, the 08:47 from Brighton, was running 15 minutes late. It hit the bus, a sixty-nine-seat 'Queen Mary', pushing it 54 yards along the track. It caught fire and was completely burnt out. Eight bus passengers were killed in the accident. The tragedy was caused solely by the signalman, who had become confused by a lot of late-running trains. He listened to a telephone service that connects a number of boxes and thought he had heard the signalman at Goring tell the signalman at Angmering that the 08.47 was not in section. He then put his signals to 'danger' and opened the gates for the traffic that had built up considerably. The bus was the first vehicle in the queue and it started to cross. Unfortunately, the train had passed the distant at 'clear' and by the time the driver saw the home at 'danger', it was too late. The diesel in the bus ignited. The leading carriage was derailed and fire-damaged; however, the rail passengers had time to get clear and no one on the train was injured. The inquiry found the signalman totally to blame but said that the installation of automatic lifting barriers would have prevented the accident.

On 9 September, the loco bringing in the empty Bournemouth Belle stock collided heavily with the buffers at Waterloo. The Pullmans were taken back to Clapham Junction for examination and another rake of coaches off the 09:24 Bournemouth–Waterloo were hastily substituted for the Pullmans. The following day all but one of the Pullmans were back on the Belle.

Loco Movements

The year did not start well for the 10:08 York–Bournemouth train. No. 6996 *Blackwell Hall* ran short of steam at Sway so No. 76012 was sent to assist. On arrival it was found that No. 6996 was a complete failure and No. 76012 was unable to move the loco with its train, so No. 35029 *Ellerman Lines* was sent to assist from the rear and the train finally arrived at Bournemouth with three engines on the train. From later that month, a West Country was booked to take over the train from Oxford rather than the *Hall*.

Crews at Eastleigh began training on a Western Region DMU between Eastleigh, Salisbury and Woking. Units used were Nos W50083 and W56294. On 21 March a trial round trip was run from Basingstoke to Waterloo, then to Salisbury and back to Basingstoke. The three-car unit ran fast between Woking and London and back, but called at all stations south of Basingstoke. It was envisaged that these units would commence running slow trains between Basingstoke and Woking during the summer. On 3 March both two-car and three-car sets were used between Reading and Redhill due to failures of the usual tadpole units.

Two Hastings six-car units were seen in Southampton on 30 January when they were used as one of three football specials taking Crystal Palace fans to the match at Southampton. The other two were hauled by Type 3 diesels.

Type 4 diesel No. D67 was trialled over junctions at Gloucester Road and in various sidings to test their suitability on Newhaven car-sleeper services. These trials must have been successful as 'Peaks' were used on pigeon trains from Newcastle. They were refuelled at Brighton. No. D330 reached Eastbourne on a senior citizens excursion from Manchester on 18 May. Similar excursions were in the hands of double-headed Type 2s – Nos D5403/12 from Newcastle, D5291/D7113 from Bradford and D7574/95 from Newcastle.

A number of Std Class 2 2-6-2Ts were nominally transferred to the Southern from the London Midland and booked to go from Lostock Hall to Fratton for use on the Isle of Wight, but the movements never materialised and the following month they were transferred back to London Midland stock.

Line Closures

The Minister gave his approval for the line north of Hailsham through Heathfield to Tunbridge Wells to be closed to passenger traffic from 14 June. The last regular steam train was the 09:00 Eastbourne–Tunbridge Wells on 12 June, with No. 80141 bearing the words 'Farewell to Steam – Cuckoo Flyer' on the smokebox. It was hauling four coaches and vans. Later that day No. 80144 was in charge of a six-coach special from Eastbourne to Tunbridge Wells and back. On the return journey a wreath was attached at Mayfield.

The following day a ten-coach excursion double-headed by Maunsell moguls Nos 31803 and 31411 travelled over the line with *The Wealdsman Railtour*.

In the evening the last scheduled through trains were three-car DEMUs. These were the 19:47 from Eastbourne with No. 1307, with the return journey being the 19:56 from Tonbridge–Eastbourne in the hands of No. 1303/8. The trains passed at Rotherfield. Later in the evening, No. 1303/8 formed the 21:47 to Heathfield and the 22:24 return working.

Freight services survived as far north as Heathfield three times a week, worked by a Type 3 diesel, but the line further north was closed completely. Passenger services between Eastbourne and Hailsham would be in the hands of DEMUs.

The Cranleigh line officially closed on the same date but the last train actually ran on 12 June. It was the line that linked Horsham to Guildford and got its name from the largest village on the line. Other stations on the line were Bramley & Wonersh, Baynards, Rudgwick and Slinfold. It was the only line in Surrey to be closed due to the Beeching Report, which stated that fewer than 5,000 passengers were using the line each week, with losses amounting to £46,000 per year. It was worked entirely by steam until the end. The last service train from Guildford was the 19:34, which consisted of No. 41287 with two three-car sets. An excursion had also travelled over the line that day hauled by Q1 No. 33006, which left Guildford for Horsham at 18:55, returning at 20:34. The next day No. 33006 was coupled to No. 33027 and they ran light over the line to Horsham where they took over another excursion, which had previously travelled over the Cuckoo Line, and this ten-coach train was the last train to travel over the branch. A Horsham & Guildford Direct Railway Society was formed and talks were held with British Railways with a view to operating the line as a light railway. It was envisaged that a DEMU would run on weekdays for commuters and a steam service at weekends for enthusiasts. It soon came to realise the hopelessness of its ambitions and was dissolved in August 1966.

Bournemouth West lost its train service from 6 September when all services due to end there were terminated at Bournemouth Central, with a bus service connecting the two stations. Posters on the stations stated that the closure would only be temporary but it soon became obvious from earthworks that were being carried out that this would not be the case. It was then officially announced that passenger services would be permanently withdrawn from Bournemouth West and Boscombe from 4 October.

Last of Classes

The last Qs to run were No. 30535 withdrawn from Guildford and No. 30545 withdrawn from Nine Elms, both in April.

The last S15 in service was No. 30837. It was retained after official withdrawal to run an enthusiasts' special, the LCGB's 'S15 Commemorative Railtour' on 9 January 1966.

Shed Closures

Tonbridge (74D) was closed on 4 January with the few remaining engines having to go to Tunbridge Wells. Tonbridge had lost its diesel and fuelling services a few months previously. From 1 March steam services from Eastbourne via the Cuckoo Line to Tonbridge were terminated at Tunbridge Wells and a DEMU shuttle service substituted for the onward journey.

Redhill (75B) closed in May. By that time it was home to only eighteen BR 2-6-4 tanks. Sub-sheds at Eastbourne, Tunbridge Wells and Three Bridges were also closed, sending their stock of engines via Redhill before continuing to Guildford. This meant that steam traction was virtually extinct on the Central Division.

Exmouth Junction, which had been a Southern shed before being transferred to the Western Region, closed in June.

Branksome shed closed on 2 August and was demolished shortly afterwards.

Miscellanea

On 4 January, British Railways reinvented itself and became British Rail, with a new blue livery and double arrow corporate symbol.

In October the first of a second batch of electro-diesels, No. E6007, was delivered and one of its first jobs was to haul a test train between Three Bridges and Littlehampton. The train was push-pull set No. 601. It was delivered in electric blue livery rather than the green livery of the initial six.

The 23:00 Brighton Belle was booked to stop at Haywards Heath, giving the station its first Pullman service.

Two new ferries were introduced on the Newhaven–Dieppe service; these were the SNCF-owned *Valencay* and *Villandry*.

A competition was held to name the new BR car ferry from Dover and the innovative name chosen was ... *Dover*! The vessel, capable of carrying 205 cars and 1,000 passengers, entered service in June.

The Southern Region trialled a new battery-operated hand-held lamp to supersede the traditional oil-fired variety. These trials were deemed successful and 42,000 were ordered for the national network. They had a simple on/off switch and rotary switch to opt between white, red or green light. It was estimated that the batteries would last six months with normal use.

A couple of West Countries were seen displaying their original numbers. No. 34009 *Lyme Regis* and No. 34048 *Crediton* had their smokebox numbers removed and 21C109 and 21C148 chalked in their place.

Ashford Works were responsible for the design and construction of two massive wagons for the transportation of boiler drums for new power stations. The wagons had two twelve-axled bogies with a tare weight of 128 tons capable of carrying loads of 290 tons. The boiler rode on swivelling cradles mounted on top of the bogies, which were positioned depending on the length of the boiler, with a maximum of 165 feet.

Lancing Works repaired its last coach – CK No. S5750S – on 11 March. By that time the place was very rundown with all the sidings to the paint shop lifted. There were still two steam locos on site – Nos DS235 and DS236, both USA 0-6-0Ts, with only the latter in steam. There was also a petrol shunter, No. DS499, waiting to be taken away for scrap. The works closed completely on 25 June. One of the USA tanks, No. DS235, left under its own steam for Eastleigh, but only got as far as Fareham. The other tank, No. DS236, left three days later. They were both cut up at Eastleigh during August.

Warship Class diesels ventured into the Central Division, working school excursions from the West Country to Gatwick and Newhaven and then taking empty coaching stock to Brighton and Three Bridges.

From 1 March Reading (Southern) was transferred to the Western Region.

Steamer services between Southampton and St Malo were discontinued.

On 31 May, Dr Richard Beeching stepped down from the chairmanship of the British Railways Board, partly due to opposition within the government to his views on transport in general.

The summer of 1965 saw the reduction of more through services, with the Wolverhampton–Eastbourne being the sole survivor.

Her Majesty's train to the Derby and the Oaks at Epsom were both hauled by electric locomotive No. 20002 for the first time. This meant it arrived at a different platform, because her usual one, Platform 6, was not electrified.

Push-pull trials were held during June with an electro-diesel, No. E6006, and two 4-CIG units, Nos 7316/7. These trials left Stewarts Lane or Wimbledon Park to Portsmouth and back via Alton, Guildford and Aldershot. No. D6580 was also fitted for push-pull working and was seen with a 6-TC set No. 601 between Wimbledon Park and Basingstoke.

Polegate had been used as a wagon scrap yard since 1956, but this was closed down early in 1965, leaving a variety of stock being dumped in the Up yard.

2-BIL unit
No. 2030 runs
under the signal
box gantry at
Clapham Junction
on 29 May 1965.

On the same day
as the above image,
Q Class No. 30548
was nearing the
end of its days at
Eastleigh.

West Country
No. 34018
Axminster on
the Ocean Liner
Express enters
the tunnel at
Southampton
on 2 June.

Merchant Navy Class No. 35017 *Belgian Marine* passes Bruton on the Bristol to Weymouth line with a SLS special on 23 May.

Rain pours off the leading carriage as No. D1601 in original two-tone green livery heads a Llanelli–Bournemouth parcels train at Southampton on 4 September. (Courtesy Trevor Tupper)

Type 3 diesel No. D6566 with the last train to leave Lancing Works on 12 June. (Courtesy Edwin Wilmshurst)

A view inside Lancing
Works and the petrol
shunter No. DS499.
(Courtesy Edwin
Wilmshurst)

A view of Ryde Pier
with Class O2 No. 17
Seaview alongside a
tram. (Courtesy Ben
Brooksbank)

O2 No. 24 *Calbourne*
waits to leave Ryde
Esplanade. (Courtesy
Ben Brooksbank)

A trio of o2s at Ryde Pierhead in the summer of 1965. (Courtesy Sid Sponheimer)

Class 4 2-6-4T No. 80032 with a southbound passenger train at Horam on 4 June. (Courtesy Keith Harwood)

A close-up of the collapsed section of the gantry carrying the signal box at Clapham Junction.

The Wealdsman Railtour with a pair of Q1s, Nos 33027 and 33006, stops at Baynards for a photo opportunity.

No. 34050 *Royal Observer Corps* took the tour from London Waterloo via Guildford and Horsham to Three Bridges and then later from Haywards Heath through Hove and Steyning back to Horsham. It is photographed here at Arundel.

A new electro-diesel, No. E6001, in original green livery at Brighton. A lighter green stripe was applied to Nos E6002–6, but after that they were painted in the new blue livery. (Courtesy Edwin Wilmshurst)

Crompton Type 3
No. D6567 stands
alongside an
unidentified Jubilee
4-6-0 at Brighton,
possibly in 1965.
(Courtesy Edwin
Wilmshurst)

A 4-SUB passes
Wimbledon in August
1965. (Courtesy
Keith Harwood)

U Class No. 31799
at the coaling stage
at Redhill shed. It
was one of the class
converted from
'River' tanks and
was withdrawn
in February 1965.
(Courtesy Sid
Sponheimer)

Chapter 7

1966

Electrification of Bournemouth Line

On 13 February, colour light signalling was introduced around Guildford. The first panel box was brought into use on the South Western Division at Ash Crossing. The boxes at Aldershot Junction South, Ash station and Wanborough were closed.

Colour light signalling was also introduced between Raynes Park and Epsom, which meant that Worcester Park and Ewell West boxes closed.

On 17 April, the new signal box at Guildford was opened. This meant that the old boxes at Shalford Junction, Guildford South and Guildford Yard all closed. The re-signalling also meant that Platform 8 at Guildford was put out of action.

By June, colour light signalling between Woking and Frimley had been brought into use.

In September, colour light signals were introduced on the Down line between Eastleigh and St Denys. The following month more lights were turned on between Totton and Brockenhurst. Eastleigh panel box was introduced in two stages – on 6 November between St Denys and Winchester and the following weekend from Winchester to Waltham. This new box took the place of twelve old boxes.

Basingstoke box was brought into use on the weekend 19/20 November, making seven old boxes redundant.

Shoe clearance tests began on newly laid sections in October using an electro-diesel coupled to a motor coach from a 6-PUL.

Work began on redesigning and re-signalling Bournemouth Central in November and finished the following month. The two through lines had been lifted but the two platforms had been re-signalled for reversible working.

The power was switched on in the new conductor rails in two stages – on 12 December between Pirbright Junction–Northbrook sub-station and two days later from Northbrook–Swaythling. Trials began immediately but were not trouble-free, as a fault at a sub-station caused a loss of power at Winchfield. A special train was laid on for press and television on 15 December from Waterloo–Eastleigh and return using a 4-CEP unit.

Accidents

Fortunately there were no major accidents on the region in 1966 but it was plagued by a host of minor ones.

No. 80141 became derailed on 9 January when leaving Morden South for Clapham Junction on a milk train. It was re-railed by breakdown cranes from Nine Elms and Guildford.

In June, a shunting accident at Clapham Junction put some of the Bournemouth Belle Pullmans out of action, but there was a seamen's strike at Dover and the Golden Arrow was not running so some Pullman cars were 'borrowed'.

On 27 July, a continental boat train hauled by No. E5002 derailed while travelling at about 60 mph at Sittingbourne, blocking both lines and causing major damage to tracks. The brake van and the last eighteen vans in the twenty-four-van train became derailed and were badly damaged before the train came to a halt in four sections. Normal working was not resumed until 04:30 on 29 July. It was deduced from the evidence gathered that excessive speed was partly the cause of the derailment. The continental vans, although allowed to run at 60 mph on the Continent, were restricted to 45 mph in this country. Although it was thought that the train was travelling at nearly 60 mph, the state of the track (which was suffering from excessive wear) also played a part.

On 1 September at Eastleigh, a freight train that was being propelled was wrongly sent into the down Portsmouth loop, colliding with two DEMUs, Nos 1109/33. Luckily little damage was done to these units and they were back in service within a few days. Several wagons were badly damaged though, with the brake van suffering most.

On 20 September, No. E6037 was derailed at Clapham Junction and No. 34036 *Westward Ho!* was summoned with the Nine Elms breakdown crane.

On 28 September, a 2-HAL unit waiting at signals between Vauxhall and Waterloo was hit by Std Class 3 2-6-2T No. 82023. Fortunately the unit was empty so there were no casualties. No. 73037 attended with the crane from Nine Elms. No. 80154 hauled the EMU back to the sidings at Clapham junction while No. 82023 made it back to Nine Elms under its own steam, although it had suffered a fractured steam pipe. It was condemned a few days later.

30 September saw yet another accident when No. D6535, working a Redbridge–Feltham freight, ran through some catch points at Weston Box and finished up in an adjoining field. The first attempt to rescue it failed and it was not until 9 October that it was re-railed.

On 12 December there was a major cliff fall between Folkestone and Dover and hundreds of tons of chalk blocked the line. The 19:00 Charing Cross–Ramsgate operated by a 4-CEP ran into the rubble, derailing it. No passengers were hurt. It took two days to remove the chalk and the line was closed again on 18 December to allow engineers to remove some overhanging boulders.

Loco Movements

The Newhaven car-sleeper, which had previously started from Glasgow, this year set off from Stirling. It ran three times each week behind Type 4 diesels from Holbeck, Leeds. Nos D25/6/9/31 had all been seen at the port.

Type 4 diesels were also to be seen in Kent operating the Ramsgate–Nottingham service.

Two unusual engines visited the region in August on rail tour duties – the first was No. 70004 *William Shakespeare* and the other was ex-LNER A2 No. 60532 *Blue Peter*.

No. 4472 *Flying Scotsman* made a visit to the region on 17 September when it hauled an enthusiasts' special from Victoria via Brighton to Eastleigh.

On 20 August, 9F No. 92002 was also spotted working the 10.54 Poole–Newcastle, made up of eleven coaches.

The winter timetable saw a resurgence of steam from Waterloo as much of the passenger stock was still only capable of being steam-heated.

A Royal train from Uckfield to Merthyr Vale on 28 October brought an unusual visitor to the region in the shape of No. D1054 *Western Governor*. Another of the class, No. D1019 *Western Challenger*, was standing by at Lewes. The train, consisting of seven vehicles, left Uckfield travelling south to Lewes and then via Haywards Heath and Kensington before joining the Western Region.

On 8 October, No. DS239, formerly C Class No. 31592, was shunting in Ashford Wagon works sporting a small wreath on its smokebox and an inscription stating that was its last day working for BR.

Line Closures

Passenger services ended on the Fawley branch and the last train was the 16:48 Fawley–Portsmouth Harbour on 11 February. It was operated by DEMU No. 1128 and according to local press reports was full of enthusiasts mourning the passing of the line. Freight traffic survived.

On the Isle of Wight, the last service from Cowes operated on Sunday 20 February. It was the 20:35 to Ryde Esplanade and was operated by No. W14 *Fishbourne*. The return working at 21:39 was in the hands of No. W22 *Brading*. Crowds gathered to witness the passing of the line but got drenched by a thunderstorm, which, ironically, closed the Cowes–Newport road due to flooding. Freight traffic survived for a while to serve Medina Wharf. The remaining line to Shanklin still needed ten duties to operate it on summer Saturdays and recent withdrawals had left only eleven engines still in service, so it was cutting it fine to say the least.

The line through Steyning closed on 6 March. A steam special that was supposed to traverse the line on 20 February never materialised, which meant that the last steam working over the line took place on 5 December 1965. The line stayed open from Shoreham to Beeding Cement Works.

3 September saw the closure of Southampton Terminus and Northam stations, with the last trains being the 22.23 Winchester City–Southampton Terminus and the 22:55 return trip. This was operated by a Hampshire diesel unit. Earlier in the day the last steam engine, BR Class 4 No. 76061, left on the 16:02 to Bournemouth Central. There was not a large turnout of enthusiasts and the police that had been drafted in to control the crowds were not needed. After the terminus closed all services were terminated at Southampton Central and initially this led to a great deal of chaos. This station also underwent rebuilding, which led to the demolition of the famous square clock tower.

Last of Classes

The last three Q1s, Nos 33006, 33020 and 33027, were withdrawn from Guildford shed (70C).

No. 31408 was the last N Class to be withdrawn in June, as was No. 31791, the last of the U Classes rebuilt from River Class tanks.

The last of the 6-PUL units were withdrawn, with the last one working on 24 April. They had spent their lives working from Victoria or London Bridge to Eastbourne, Hastings and Worthing. Many of the coaches lived on in 6-COR units (Nos 3041–50) reformed in 1965. The displaced Pullmans had replaced some restaurant cars in 4-RES units, making 'new' 4-PUL units. Many of the Pullmans, including *Anne*, *Violet*, *Ethel*, *May*, *Ida*, *Naomi* and *Joyce*, had been sent to Messrs A. King & Sons of Wymondham for scrapping. Eight 'new' 4-COR units (Nos 3161–3168) were reformed from disbanded 4-PUL and 4-COR sets.

Sheds Closed

Feltham shed closed in October. By that time, this once busy shed only had an allocation of 4 Class 4 BR 2-6-4 tanks – Nos 80033/68/85/140. It continued to operate as a diesel depot.

Southampton Docks also closed. The allocation of shunters Nos D2986–97 was transferred to Eastleigh.

By 1966 the tracks at Brighton shed – which had closed in 1964 – had been lifted and the turntable removed. Two sidings remained alongside the old shed for berthing of diesels.

Miscellanea

BR applied for an Act of Parliament to reinstate the Hamsey loop north of Lewes. This would mainly follow the original route from Lewes to Uckfield and do away with the difficult route out of Lewes that crossed the High Street over a bridge. This new line was never built but at the time of writing is still part of a new proposal for a second route from Brighton to London.

As an economy measure, it was announced that Shoreham station in Kent would close at 20:15. This led to many protests, and a group of twelve commuters on the first train scheduled not to stop, the 19:48 Holborn Viaduct–Sevenoaks, threatened to pull the communication cord. An SR official on the train ordered the driver to stop in the interests of safety, but took the particulars of all the troublesome commuters. Subsequently, meetings took place where it was argued that there were another forty SR stations used less in the evenings that were staying open and the commuters won the argument and the stop was reinstated. The economies sought, however, were gained by closing the station in the afternoons!

Three nameplates from Bulleid Pacifics were presented to the Canadian Railroad Historical Association. These were *Canadian Pacific, Cunard White Star* and *Dorchester*. Lord Dorchester had once been Governor General of Canada.

A new station opened at Southampton Airport on 1 April. It had no road access or ticket office, with tickets having to be purchased from an airline office.

Posters were displayed at a number of London stations, including Waterloo, urging passengers to use Paddington if they wished to travel to the West Country. Summer Saturday departures were reduced from previous years, with booking recommended for all seats on the morning departures of express services to Salisbury and Sidmouth Junction. The 11:00 departure, which had once been the ACE, was by then reduced to a Western DEMU to Salisbury calling at Woking.

The first of the tube trains converted at Acton Works to third rail for use on the Isle of Wight ran under 'its own steam' for the first time when it went from Wimbledon Park to Stewarts Lane on 16 May. They were to be classified as 4-VEC and 3-TIS – very apt for the island. Crew training took place at the end of June at Stewarts Lane. Conductor rail for the electrification on the island was taken from Redbridge Works to Medina Wharf by barge and then by rail to where it was needed. By August most of the rail was lying in place on the trackside. It was envisaged that the line to Shanklin would close on 31 December and re-open in April 1967 using the new electrified ex-tube stock.

The electrification of the main line to Bournemouth meant various diversions were put in place over weekends when work was being carried out. At the end of April trains were diverted over the Mid-Hants line through Alton. On Sunday 24 April the Down Bournemouth Belle was double-headed by a Type 3 diesel piloting No. 34017 *Ilfracombe* but the following Sunday a Type 4 diesel, No. D1686, was used, negating the need for another loco. The Up trains on both days were worked by Stanier Class 5 No. 45493, which had reached Bournemouth the previous day by working the 10:08 York–Poole. There were a couple of days during the summer when planned electrification works had to be cancelled due of a shortage of guards required to work on the ballast trains.

The Southern Region borrowed an inspection saloon from the Eastern Region so that 200 invited commuters could see how electrification work was progressing. Only twelve could travel at any time in its armchairs and it was attached to the 07:24 Bournemouth Central–Waterloo and the 16:35 return trip.

The Preservation Society on Hayling Island was dealt a blow when a contract was awarded for the demolition of the swing bridge on the Langstone Viaduct. BR was under a statutory obligation to open the swing bridge for any passing vessel. Vandals had removed the decking, leading to the windlass that operated the bridge denying access and making the bridge inoperable. The bridge had also reached the end of its working life, so removal was the only option, allowing members of the Langstone Sailing Club to gain access to their boatyard. The Preservation Society seemed unperturbed by this as they knew the bridge needed replacing and BR would now have to meet the cost of dismantling it.

A new 'Seaspeed' hovercraft service was introduced to the Isle of Wight on 6 July. It left the mainland at Crosshouse Road, Southampton going to Medina Road, Cowes.

The journey took 20 minutes. In the first week of service some Royal Mail was carried between the two locations, with special postmarks being applied to commemorate the event.

DEMU No. 1103 was the first of the class to be painted in the new blue livery, with No. 1109 being the last to receive a coat of green paint. Other units that were the first to be outshopped in blue were Nos 3124, 5215/9/43, and 6006/20/36.

In August a couple of cheap excursions costing 10/- (50p) were run from South London to coastal resorts, which proved extremely popular. The first to Littlehampton from Streatham Hill, Norwood and Sutton attracted over 2,000 passengers. These filled two special trains and the rest had to use service trains. These numbers were swelled by the sunny weather, but a week later, in less welcoming weather, 1,300 made the journey to Bognor on two special trains.

By November, the Pullman brakes on the Bournemouth Belle had been taken off and replaced by BKs in blue livery.

The Swanage Branch was dieselised at the start of the winter service on 5 September. The service from Wareham was operated by a single Hampshire DEMU, which left the Lymington Branch being the only steam-operated branch on the region. 'Southern' locos had long since disappeared though and the service was in the hands of BR Class 2 2-6-2Ts or Class 4 2-6-4Ts.

On 3 October, No. 34089 *602 Squadron* was the last steam locomotive to be repaired at Eastleigh Works. Later that month, on Sunday 23rd, there were still thirty-nine steam locos and seventeen diesels on shed, including No. D3464 in blue livery. On the same date, at Salisbury, there were seven WC/BBs and four various Stds.

SR's announcement of their intention to close the branch from Appledore through Lydd to New Romney brought loud protests from the latter's town council. BR informed the council that they could bid to buy the line if they wished and this seemed to have quietened their protestations.

No. E6043 was used to check clearances within Southampton Docks in November. At that time, Brush Type 4s were banned from both Eastern and Western Docks.

In December, the freight service between Folkestone and Boulogne was withdrawn as it was totally uneconomic. The ship operating the service, *Brest*, was to find work on the Channel Islands route. Locals in Folkestone accused BR of deliberately running the service down while yet refusing to sell it to interested private companies. BR said that this was because had been carrying out a feasibility study to see whether it could become a hovercraft terminal, but the results of this study were not favourable.

The youth hanging from the cab side is believed to be the author. A group of pals and I bought an all-line Southern Region Rail Rover in the summer of 1966 and on at least one occasion travelled from our home town of Eastbourne to the Isle of Wight. In the sidings and obviously out of service was an unidentified O2. Behind is No. 24 *Calbourne*. (Below): On the same trip was No. 17 *Seaview* ready to leave Ryde Esplanade. Both photographs were taken with a Box Brownie, so are not the best quality.

No. 34089 *602 Squadron* storms south through Balcombe on a wet 10 December with an LCGB Reunion Railtour to Brighton and Kemp Town.

No. 34032 *Camelford* looks to be in pretty good external condition at Bournemouth shed in April. (Courtesy Sid Sponheimer)

A trio of O2s at Ryde shed, with No. 24 *Calbourne* minus nameplate having its smokebox cleaned out. (Courtesy Sid Sponheimer)

Low tide at Ryde
as an unidentified
silhouetted O2
heads along the
pier. (Courtesy Sid
Sponheimer)

350 hp shunter
No. 15232 was at
Fratton shed in March
1966. It had been
built at Ashford in
1949. (Courtesy Keith
Harwood)

Three-car Hampshire
DMU No. 1125 at
Medstead and Four
Marks on the now
preserved Mid-Hants
Railway. (Courtesy
Keith Harwood)

An unidentified
4-LAV passes through
Wivelsfield on a London
Bridge–Brighton via
Redhill stopping service
on 17 September.
(Courtesy Edwin
Wilmshurst)

Early days on the
Bluebell and ex-LNWR
No. 2650 coupled to a
SECR birdcage coach in
1966. The loco had been
withdrawn from traffic
in 1960 and stored at
Derby before being
sold to the Bluebell in
1962 for £890. It was
hired to contractors and
was used to help lift
the track from Horsted
Keynes to Ardingly and
East Grinstead.

A view of Eastbourne's
goods yard. The centre
road with the 4-LAV
on has since been lifted.
The Drewry shunter
was a common sight
during the 1960s. The
goods shed in the centre
of the photo is now a
shopping centre.

Another view of Eastbourne on 24 April when an LCGB railtour to celebrate the passing of the 6-PUL/6-PAN units visited the town as well as Hastings, Seaford and Brighton. No. 3041 was photographed at Platform 4, which has since been lifted to make way for a ring road.

A wintry scene: Guildford shed on 23 January with a Maunsell Mogul on the turntable. (Courtesy Keith Harwood)

Drewry shunter No. D2294 at Eastleigh shed in the summer on 1966. (Courtesy Keith Harwood)

No. E6046 as delivered in blue livery
with yellow panel at Clapham Junction.
(Courtesy Keith Harwood)

A 4-COR waits at Waterloo with a
Portsmouth and Southsea via Bookham
train while a WR diesel-hydraulic
Warship Class awaits its next duty in
the background.

Britannia Class No. 70004 *William
Shakespeare* minus nameplates passes
Vauxhall on its way back to Waterloo
heading the A2 Commemorative Railtour
on 14 August 1967.

Chapter 8

1967

Bournemouth Electrification

The line from Basingstoke to Bournemouth was electrified this year. On 18 January the power was switched on between Swaythling and the Lymington branch and a test train ran consisting of two 2-EPB units coupled to an electro-diesel.

Colour light signalling was switched on at the end of February between Lymington Junction and Christchurch, meaning the closure of signal boxes at Sway, New Milton and Hinton Admiral. Earlier in the month the area covered by Basingstoke box was extended to Andover, closing Overton and Whitchurch North boxes. These new sections were the last to be switched on before the new electric service started. The Surbiton–Woking section was scheduled to be turned on after the service had started.

In March the section between Bournemouth Central and Branksome was energised, including the carriage sidings.

Southampton Central station was redesigned and one casualty was the famous clock tower that had overlooked the site for seventy years. In its place was a new building comprising of ticket hall, information office, refreshment room, bookstall and toilets.

In order to convert to electrification, new sheds had to be built to house and maintain the new units. Bournemouth West was closed on 4 October 1965 and the sheds were built on what were the approaches to the old terminus.

The first 4-REP, No. 3001, started trials on 10 February when it ran a circular trip from Stewarts Lane via Clapham Junction, Twickenham, Kingston, Wimbledon and East Putney. It then performed high-speed trials on the Eastern Division. By the end of the month it was coupled to TC (Trailer Control) units Nos 402/3 for trials to Basingstoke.

Also that month, shoe clearance trials were being carried out between Brockenhurst–Bournemouth Central using No. E6043, a withdrawn 6-PAN motor coach from unit No. 3031, and a brake van.

The first 4-VEP (Vestibule Electro-Pneumatic), No. 7701, arrived at Stewarts Lane from Derby during March. These high capacity units that had three and two side-by-side seating had been ordered from BR workshops in York to operate stopping services. More were subsequently ordered, with the last ones being introduced in 1974 after a total of 194 units had been delivered. Their numbers were later altered to 3001–3194.

Some electric services started between Waterloo and Bournemouth on 3 April, with two duties using 4-REP units, Nos 3001/3, and four duties using electro-diesels, with TC sets working push-pull trains, but the first full service using electric multiple units operated on 10 July 1967, the day after the last steam engine ran. The first train to arrive at Bournemouth was powered by a 4-REP (Restaurant Electro-Pneumatic) coupled to TC units. There were fifteen REPs built at BR's workshops at York. They were originally classified as Class 430s and numbered 3001–15, later to become Class 432s and were renumbered 2001–15. There were three 3TC units and twenty-four 4TC units also built at York. Only the 4-REP was a powered unit and was powerful enough to propel the other units. The REP units had eight traction motors each and produced 3,200 hp, which was only 100 hp less than a Deltic. (It was not possible join two 4-REPs together without isolating some motors as these would overload the circuits.) The 4-REPs were always marshalled at the London end of the train as the section from Bournemouth to Weymouth was not electrified as it was not financially viable to do so. The two power cars in each 4-REP unit were new-built vehicles but the buffets were rebuilt from loco-hauled buffets dating back to 1961 and kept much of the original interiors, while the other intermediate vehicles were converted from Mk1 Trailer Brake Firsts. All the TC units were converted from BR MK1 loco-hauled stock originally classified as Class 491/2 before becoming Class 438.

From Bournemouth the 4-REP was uncoupled and the TC units were coupled to a Class 33 that had been converted to push-pull operation to continue the journey to Weymouth. These were reclassified as Class 33/1s. On the return journey the coaches were propelled to Bournemouth where the 4-REP was reattached for the onward journey to Waterloo.

Bournemouth station was redesigned with the two through roads being taken up and replaced with berthing sidings.

The track was energised on the Lymington Branch on 1 June, with a trial train being run on the same day.

Southampton Terminus and Northam stations were not included in the electrification scheme and were closed, but Southampton Docks were still served by the electric trains being hauled there by Class 73 or 74 electro-diesels.

The early days of operations were not entirely successful due to the late delivery of some units from BR's workshops at York, and in the first few weeks of operation there was a fairly high failure rate and many trains were either loco-hauled or were formed of fewer coaches than they were scheduled to be. As buffet facilities were only available in 4-REPs, if one of these units failed then all catering services were also lost. It was well into 1968 before 100 per cent of the service was in the hands of the EMUs.

When they first appeared they were in all-over blue livery with a yellow square on either end. They also had an aluminium BR emblem on cab doors. In the late 1960s they were repainted into the new corporate blue/grey livery with all-yellow ends and they lost their aluminium insignia. No. 2111 was the first unit to be so-treated.

The first electric service from Waterloo–Basingstoke had started on 2 January with the first train being the 07.27 from Basingstoke, which was made up of four 2-HAP sets with No. 6088 at the front and a 2-EPB, No. 5673, making a ten-car train.

Electric stock could now reach Eastleigh but SUBs, LAVs, BILs and HALs had to have their heating and lighting circuits cut out from Pirbright Junction.

The first revenue-earning electric train to reach Southampton Central was on 1 April when a special train consisting of two 4-CEP units, Nos 7122/74, ran from Folkestone Harbour with an Italian crew of a ship.

The introduction of electric services obviously meant a reduction in steam-hauled trains and by April there were only eight into and out of Waterloo each day. These included Channel Island boat trains to Weymouth.

A more powerful type of electro-diesel than the Class 73 Nos E6001–49 was needed so it was decided to convert ten of the E5XXX series. They were numbered E6101–10. The extra space required to install the diesel engine was acquired by removing the large flywheel needed to keep these locos moving over breaks in conductor rails. They produced 2,550 hp using their electric motors compared to the E6XXX series 1,600 hp and generated another 50 hp on their diesel engines.

Isle of Wight

The conductor rails on the Isle of Wight were energised on 1 March and the service using the converted 4-VEC and 3-TIS units started on the 20th. In all there were forty-two cars converted from 1920s LT stock.

London Bridge Area Re-Signalling

To help speed up the service in this congested area, major re-signalling and track work was carried out on the approaches to London Bridge and new crossovers were installed at both London Bridge and Cannon Street stations. A new connection was laid at Metropolitan Junction, which enabled empty coaching stock to move directly between Cannon Street and Blackfriars without interfering with the service trains between London Bridge and Waterloo East.

End of Steam

1967 saw the end of steam operation on the Southern Region. At the start of the year there were 122 steam engines still in service allocated to seven sheds as follows: Nine Elms (70A) twenty-seven locos, Guildford (70C) thirteen locos, Eastleigh (70D) thirty-three locos, Salisbury (70E) twelve locos, Bournemouth (70F) twenty-one locos, Weymouth (70G) fourteen locos, and Ryde (70H) two locos.

The USA tank No. DS233 that shunted Redbridge sleeper works was replaced by a Drewry shunter on 6 March.

Bournemouth Belle

The last Bournemouth Belle ran on 9 July. Although it was by now rostered as a diesel turn, steam had put in appearances during the last week, including runs by No. 34024 *Tamar Valley*, No. 34025 *Whimple* and No. 34036 *Westward Ho!* Steam traction had been diagrammed for the last ever run but this was altered at the last moment and it operated behind a grimy Type 4 No. D1924. The trip, which had been heavily booked by enthusiasts, suffered several last-minute cancellations.

Accidents

A serious accident occurred near Hither Green on 5 November when a twelve-car train consisting of units Nos 1007/17 making up the 19:43 Hastings–Charing Cross derailed while travelling at 70 mph. The leading pair of wheels of the third coach hit a piece of broken rail and derailed. It stayed upright until it reached a diamond crossing, which caused the coach in front to derail and coaches two to five to overturn. The coupling behind the leading coach broke and it carried on unharmed, stopping about 200 yards further on. It was a Sunday evening and there were many passengers standing in the corridors. Forty-nine people were killed with another twenty-seven seriously injured. Thirty-three ambulances attended and the first casualty arrived at hospital within 18 minutes of the accident occurring. Twenty-eight fire engines attended as well as the Salvation Army and the WRVS. Robin Gibb of the Bee Gees was travelling on the train but was not injured. The derailment was put down to poor track conditions and speed limits were reduced from 75 mph to 60 mph.

The wreckage was cleared and all running lines reopened by 15:40 on 7 November. In comparison, at Lewisham on 24 January 2017 a freight train overturned and it took almost a week to resume normal service.

On 22 January, while helping with the removal of track at Steyning, shunter No. D3219 became derailed at the south end of the station and No. D6556 was summoned with the breakdown crane to re-rail it.

On 28 March the rear coach of 4-EPB, No. 5129, became derailed when entering Waterloo on the 09:10 from Guildford, blocking Platforms 1–7 and thereby causing chaos. Normal service could not be restored until 20:45 that evening. Many services during the day had to be terminated at Clapham Junction or Wimbledon.

On 17 May the Hoo Junction–Snowdown Colliery freight was derailed at Faversham at 04:45 while being shunted, blocking the line to Sittingbourne. The line was cleared later that morning.

On 17 July a collision occurred at Maidstone East station when the 15:54 Maidstone East–Victoria made up of two 2-HAP units was hit from behind by a freight train. The latter was the 15:28 Class 5 from Ashford–Willesden, headed by No. E5010 and hauling twenty-six loaded continental ferry vans. The force of the collision shunted the passenger train forward 76 feet, causing slight injuries to thirteen passengers. The collision was put down to two reasons. Firstly, only six of the vans were vacuum-braked and to make it a Class 5, a minimum of 50 per cent (14 per cent on this train) should have been fitted. Secondly, the weight of the train had been underestimated by the guard. Despite this, subsequent tests concluded that the train could have stopped if it had been adhering to the speed limit. However, using actual times that the train had passed signal boxes, it was concluded that the speed was in excess of 60 mph, which was more than 10 mph over the speed limit.

Some vans became derailed while being shunted at Clapham Junction on 19 June. This blocked the local Windsor lines and blocked in stock for two West of England expresses, leading to their cancellation.

Faversham witnessed a derailment on 24 October. The 11.45 Queenborough–Ashford empty coal wagons were being shunted backwards when the train was wrongly shunted into a siding and was unable to stop before crashing through the buffers. The guard managed to jump clear before his van came to a sudden stop, with the wagons behind it rearing up. Metal from buffers was torn off and thrown into the entrance of the subway, causing some damage.

On 28 November, the 03:40 paper train, hauled by No. E6101 from Waterloo–Farnborough, derailed at Raynes Park, blocking all the lines. The investigation uncovered that seven of the wagons were Vanfits, restricted to 45 mph, and were only on the train due to a shortage of suitable vehicles. It was the responsibility of the guard to inform the driver of this, but he failed to do so. This may have been partly because his driver was on a spare duty and was only given about 15 minutes' notice that a driver had failed to turn up for work and he was required to work this train. Although he walked past the wagons to reach his cab, he failed to recognise that these seven wagons, marshalled 9–15 in the train, were unsuitable for high-speed running. Diversions had to be put into place throughout the day, with main line services being sent via Chertsey and Windsor, and some Portsmouth services were diverted into Victoria. Most of the services were back to normal in time for the evening rush hour.

Loco Movements

In June, A4 No. 4498 *Sir Nigel Gresley* operated a couple of rail tours out of Waterloo. On 3 June it visited Bournemouth, Southampton and Salisbury. The following day it worked a return trip to Weymouth.

The Southern ran two 'Farewell to Steam' specials from Waterloo on Sunday 2 July. One was behind No. 35008 *Orient Line* with eleven coaches that went to Weymouth, and No. 35028 *Clan Line* that went to Bournemouth with a rake of ten coaches. Response to these tours had been relatively poor and it was originally intended to run five trips but it is believed that the high price put people off buying tickets. Poor publicity was also blamed for the low uptake.

The last steam working into Waterloo was by No. 35030 *Elder Dempster Lines*, which arrived with the 14:11 ex-Weymouth.

During the last week of operation many of the remaining steam engines found their way to Salisbury or Weymouth for storage, awaiting disposal. At the end of the month there were forty-six engines at Salisbury and twenty-one at Weymouth. A few remained at Nine Elms with the last two, No. 34084 *253 Squadron* and No. 35023 *Holland-Afrika Line*, being towed away on Sunday 10 September.

An LNER K4, No. 3442 *The Great Marquess*, visited Brighton and Chichester on its way to Southampton with an enthusiasts' tour from Victoria on 12 March. On the return journey the loco came off at Clapham Junction and went to Nine Elms and a Class 33 took the train from there back to Victoria.

Eastbourne and Brighton had a final visit of a steam loco on 19 March with the 'Southern Rambler' rail tour. It was in the hands of filthy No. 34108 *Wincanton*, which was a last-minute substitute for a failed No. 34089 *602 Squadron*.

An unusual sight on the Oxted lines occurred on 30 July when two specials were run from Norwich and Lowestoft with army cadets heading for Crowborough. They were in the hands of D5630 and D5682.

Brush Type 2s were appearing on through freights in North Kent. Locos noted included Nos D5504/8/11/51/3/6/75/7. Nos D6701/7/22 also put in appearances.

More Brush Type 4s were being allocated to the region and were appearing on West of England trains from Waterloo and occasionally on the Pines Express.

Line Closures

On 2 January, the line between Three Bridges to East Grinstead was closed.

The New Romney branch closed on 6 March, two months later than envisaged, as there had been disagreement between the Traffic Commissioners and Minister of Transport over the level of proposed alternative bus services. The last train from New Romney left at 22:38 and although normally consisted of empty coaching stock, passengers were allowed aboard and around fifty people took advantage of a ride to Ashford. The line remained opened as far as Dungeness and the need to remove nuclear waste has probably gone some way to retaining the Hastings–Ashford line. At the time, though, the future of the line looked bleak. The bridge outside Rye was broken and had a 5 mph speed limit over it. The cuttings east of Ore were also slowly encroaching onto the track.

Shed Closures

On 9 July, Nine Elms (70A), Guildford (70C), Salisbury (70E) and Weymouth (70G) closed completely. On the same date the following closed to steam – Feltham (70B), Eastleigh (70D), and Bournemouth (70F).

Miscellanea

More units were being painted in blue livery, with Nos 1106/13 being early examples. Shunters started to appear from Ashford Works in blue livery, with one of the first being No. D4100. Some coaches were beginning to appear in a blue/grey livery.

The last of the electro-diesels, No. E6049, was delivered in January.

On 13 January the 17:47 London Bridge–Portsmouth service was inadvertently switched to an unelectrified line at Redhill. Luckily it came to a halt with one pick-up shoe still in contact with the third rail and it was possible to reverse up.

On 21 January the Minister of Transport ordered an inquiry into the safety of the line that ran under the chalk cliffs between Folkestone and Dover. There was another cliff fall on the 26th of the month near Abbott's Cliff Tunnel, causing the line to be closed. It was re-opened the following day with trains passing with extreme caution. The line was closed again for the first three days of February, so more potentially dangerous chalk could be removed from the cliffs.

The Pines Express ceased running on 4 March. The Up train was worked by No. D1700 and the Down train by No. D1653. It had been diverted away from the Somerset & Dorset line in September 1962 and re-routed via Basingstoke and Oxford. New services introduced in its place were the 08:38 Southampton Central and the 16:21 Poole, both to Birmingham New Street. There were two return journeys, both starting from New Street – the 09:40 to Poole and the 17:40 to Southampton Central, but the direct link with Manchester was lost.

There was still a through service from Poole to York, which was scheduled to be diesel-hauled, but due to several failures steam could still be occasionally seen working this train as far as Reading General.

A new weekly freight service from Cornwall to Sittingbourne started. It was called 'The Clayfreighter', carrying clay slurry in liquid form for use in the Sittingbourne paper mills. It was pumped directly from the tankers into the mill's own tanks. Previously, it had to be dried before it was transported and was then re-liquefied on arrival at the mill.

The last scheduled steam service on the Lymington Branch was on 2 April. The branch, which had been the last preserve of the M7s, and more recently Ivatt Class 2 2-6-2Ts and BR 2-6-4Ts, had been the last steam-operated branch on the Southern.

A letter, posted in Jamaica, addressed to 'The Bridge School, First second class carriage on the 08.45 Haywards Heath–London Bridge train', was handed over by the station manager. It was from one of the former members of the school to his companions.

The 'Hornbys', Nos 20001/2/3, were taken off one of their regular duties, the Victoria–Newhaven boat trains, and were replaced by a blue electro-diesel heading a set of blue/grey-painted stock.

The first assignment of atomic waste arrived at Newhaven from power stations at Harwell and Aldermaston on 17 May. It was transferred to the MV *Topaz*, which took it to the mid-Atlantic and dumped it!

Despite the rundown of steam and poor external condition of the remaining WC/BBs and MNs, some impressive speeds of over 90 mph were still regularly being recorded, with 95 mph being obtained by No. 34036 *Westward Ho!* at Waller's Ash in June. The same loco stopped at Poole to await assistance up Parkstone Bank while on a heavy boat train from Weymouth on bank holiday Monday 29 May. When it became evident that no assistance was available, the driver decided to tackle the 1 in 60 climb unaided. The sound was said to be spectacular and it managed to reach the top of the incline at 18 mph.

A new freightliner depot was built at Millbrook Yard at Southampton and was the first to be built on the Southern.

British Railways was growing increasingly hostile to running steam specials. The Western Region had already banned them entirely and other areas were showing more reluctance, stating that fuelling, manning and inspecting steam engines was becoming increasingly difficult and any profits did not make up for the fact that organising these trips distracted managers from their main business of running a modern railway.

In the first year of operating hovercraft across The Solent, Seaspeed's two SRN6 vessels carried over 100,000 passengers and over 5,000 articles of freight. An availability rate of over 96 per cent had been obtained and a new type, the HM2, was to be ordered.

For the skiing season, a through service to Basle was started. It was achieved by attaching another carriage to the 21:00 Night Ferry. This carriage would be detached at Lille and attached to a buffet car express arriving at the resort at 14:18.

Electric units were beginning to appear, with their whole ends completely painted yellow rather than just having a yellow panel. Units 2-HAL No. 2663 and 4-EPB No. 5165 were spotted with complete yellow ends but having been given a new coat of green, rather than blue, paint.

The first batch of 4-VEPs intended for use on the Brighton line to replace the 4-LAVs were transferred to the Western Division to make up for the chronic shortage of available stock.

The first units to appear in the new blue/grey livery were 4-CEPs Nos 7143/56 being seen at Durnsford Road in August, and 4-BIG No. 7035 in September.

Excursions were by now mainly in the hands of multiple units. A group of students travelled from Bournemouth to Dover Marine with a 4-VEP for motive power. On three occasions in August, excursions were run by the WR from Reading to Margate using DEMUs. An exception to this was three excursions from the WR to Eastbourne on 27 August, where they were all headed by Type 4s Nos D1599, D1732 and D1929.

A programme of 'Holiday Week' specials ran from Eastbourne commencing 7 August and included a boat trip. They called at Lewes and Brighton before progressing to Hampton Court for Richmond, Portsmouth Harbour for Ryde, and Windsor for Runnymede. A 4-COR was used throughout the week.

Another familiar scene fast disappearing from stations was the waving of a green flag by the guard. This was being replaced by a buzzer above his door that rang in the driver's cab.

The line north of Heathfield was being lifted at the start of November. The shunter No. D3669 from Eastbourne took the demolition train on a nightly run up the line to Argos Hill Tunnel north of Mayfield, and it was the first train to travel over the line in over two years. On 7 November it became derailed at Mayfield. As soon as the line had been lifted as far as Heathfield, the remaining section would be lifted with demolition trains arriving from the north.

Railway World published an article on how they thought the Southern had been run during 1967. It was not exactly complimentary. Although they conceded that the new timetable had been well thought out and planned, it fell down because it depended on an unrealistic figure for stock availability. It also criticised the fact that route numbers had changed on the same day as timetable changes and drivers had not been fully briefed on these changes. When things did go awry, the public were not informed of what was happening – sometimes because the staff did not know themselves. The magazine staff pointed out how some delays could escalate from minor events. From their offices at Shepperton, they often noticed that the driver was not looking as the guard flagged the train away, so they had to resort to flashing the train lights on/off to attract the driver's attention. This 2 or 3-minute delay would escalate if the train had then missed its path. Early snow and ice in December also caused chaos, with ice forming on conductor rails and frozen snow blocking points. There are solutions to these problems but they, of course, cost money, so had not been implemented.

No. 34100 *Appledore* with smokebox number chalked on enters Southampton Central on 7 May.

No. E6039 passes
through Woking on
a crew training run.
(Courtesy Trevor
Tupper)

DMU No. 1114
at Isfield with a
southbound train
to Lewes. The black
triangle denotes that
the guards van is at this
end of the unit. This
was to assist postmen
waiting on platforms
for approaching trains
so they could position
themselves for loading
sacks when the train
stopped. (Courtesy
Keith Harwood)

Type 3 No. D6588
at Newark on 28
September, with new
units Nos 7721/2 being
delivered from BR
workshops at York.

4-EPB No. 5010 on a Windsor–
Waterloo via Richmond service
at Datchet on 5 February.
(Courtesy Keith Harwood)

4-CEP No. 7136 was one
of the first units to appear
in blue/grey livery and was
photographed at Chichester on
a Portsmouth–Victoria service
on 23 September. (Courtesy
Trevor Tupper)

No. E5016 passes through
Ashford with a freight train
in September. (Courtesy
Robert Carroll)

Chapter 9

1968

The Southern's first freightliner depot opened at Millbrook, Southampton, on 29 January, although trials had begun a week earlier. There was only one train per day when it opened and this was the 17:39 SX to Stratford in the hands of a Brush Type 4. A second service was initiated the next week with a train to Dudley again using a Brush Type 4. This service was worked on alternate days by Eastleigh and Gateshead locomotives.

The 4-REPS had gained a poor reputation in 1967 for losing pick-up shoes and 1968 did not bring an improvement, with No. 3001 losing one near West Byfleet while working a Bournemouth–Waterloo train. In March, Nos 3008, 3002 and 3006 all lost shoes and their journeys had to be terminated early.

The ex-Pullman Works at Brighton were being used to store preserved steam engines. Early in the morning of 23 January, Nos 45000 and 92220 arrived, having been towed from Stafford. Later in the month Nos 30245, 30850, 30925 and 120 also arrived. In March Nos 33001, 30777, 70000 and 42500 added to the collection, but the latter two were moved away during December.

On 24 August another train left Stewarts Lane for Brighton with a diverse collection of stock. No. E6044 was in charge of Q7, LNER 0-8-0, No. 63460, a variety of coaches that included a restored LSWR tri-composite, a steam crane, an assortment of old wagons that included some ancient Stockton & Darlington wagons, and a fire engine marked 'Gateshead Loco'.

Accidents

At a Continental-type level crossing at Ash on 2 January, the 11:05 Ramsgate–Charing Cross train hit a breakdown lorry. The train was travelling at about 55 mph. The barriers were down, but the lorry driver swerved around them. The driver of the truck and his son were killed.

On 3 January a train hit a fallen tree near Sutton station. There were no injuries but passengers had to de-train and walk about 100 yards along the track to the station.

On 9 January a four-car EMU derailed at Selsdon, blocking the line between South Croydon and Sanderstead for the evening rush hour.

On 15 February at Wimbledon 4-SUB No. 4365 on the 12:14 Waterloo–Effingham Junction ran into the rear of 4-SUB No. 4625 on the 12:06 Waterloo–Chessington

South standing at the platform. The cab of No. 4365 was badly damaged. Six passengers were slightly injured and the guard suffered concussion.

On 6 March the 08:45 Poole–Broadstone freight derailed while leaving Poole yard, blocking both Up and Down lines.

A more serious derailment of a freight train occurred on 18 March when a train of Prestflo cement wagons became derailed when travelling near New Milton, on a Poole–Plymouth freight. The train crew did not realise this immediately and carried on. When it did become evident, 1,500 concrete sleepers were so badly damaged that they needed replacing. The conductor rail and many insulators also needed replacing.

On 11 July, a derailment occurred at Waterloo when the rear motor coach of 4-REP No. 3006 and the first three coaches of 4-TC No. 301 were leaving Platform 9 with the 11:47 for Bournemouth, resulting in five platforms being blocked for the rest of the day.

Another derailment of an electric unit happened when 4-CEP No. 7010 came off the tracks when leaving the sidings at Bognor Regis on 10 July. Not only did it block the main lines, but also the level crossings.

On 1 October, Hastings unit No. 1035 working the 16:34 Tunbridge Wells–Hastings hit a lady, who fell in front of it at Robertsbridge station. It was travelling at 75 mph. The driver applied the emergency brakes and the wheels locked up, causing them to flat spot. It had to be reversed into a siding at Robertsbridge (with the wheels hammering the track) where it was taken out of service.

A child was knocked down and killed on 11 October at West Minster crossing, Sheppey. The inquest stated that the vision of both driver and child was obscured by weeds.

On 4 December, an eight-car EPB set ran away from Sevenoaks station and rolled over 3 miles before becoming derailed at Otford. There were no casualties but it caused several long delays.

On New Year's Eve at 17:15 at Norwood Junction station, an accident occurred between two eight-car electric units. The 16:57 Coulsdon North–London Bridge made up of two 4-SUB units, Nos 4280/4103, was standing at the Up local platform when it was hit by two 4-EPB units, Nos 5115/5046. This train had overrun a red light. Fifty-six passengers received minor injuries as did the drivers of both trains, while a guard suffered a broken rib. The cab of the stationary train came off far worse, being crushed back to the first compartment. The driver was held solely to blame for passing a signal at red, but more extraordinary was the fact that he had been held at a red light just outside the station (Signal CY29) while the train he hit had joined his track from Selhurst within his field of vision, so he knew it was there and should have expected to be held up again when approaching the station.

Locomotive Movements

Diesels that had brought excursions into the region were sometimes used to operate other services. On 26 May, No. D136, which had arrived with the Stirling–Newhaven car-sleeper, was commandeered to work a freight to Norwood, as was No. D1642, which had been on a Maidenhead to Brighton excursion. Both returned light to the south coast to work their return services.

The two USA tanks that had been used as departmental locomotives at Ashford, Nos DS237 and DS238, were being towed to South Wales for scrapping when they ran hot boxes and only made it as far as Tonbridge, where they stayed for several days. The Western Region refused permission for them to travel over their rails, and to finish the journey by road was too expensive. This story had a happy ending though, because they were bought by the KESR and restored.

An 8-VAB (Vestibule Autobrake Buffet), No. 8001, was produced to cover for a shortage of stock on the Waterloo–Bournemouth line. It was made up of three-car and five-car set VEP units, the latter including a buffet adapted from loco-hauled stock, and had three power cars producing 3,300 hp. The unit could not be split according to some reports, but could be attached to a 4-TC or 4-VEP unit. It regularly worked three daily return trips from Bournemouth–Waterloo until August, when it spent several weeks unused in the yard at Clapham.

By early May, nine out of ten of the Class 71s had been converted to Class 74s (Nos E6101–10) and had been used on trials and empty coaching stock workings. They had not been allowed on revenue-earning service until then and still weren't allowed on freight trains. One of their first duties was on 6 May, when No. E6106 was seen on the 13:16 Waterloo–Southampton Eastern Docks. When they did enter service they turned out to be unreliable, with a multitude of breakdowns due to a variety of reasons.

Line Closures

The freight-only service between Hailsham and Heathfield came to an abrupt halt on 26 April when a lorry hit an underbridge, causing enough damage to make running locomotives over it dangerous. There were a number of wagons stranded at Heathfield and these languished there for some time before until an engineer's petrol trolley was used to bring the wagons in ones and twos back to Hailsham, which still retained a twice-weekly freight service operated by the Drewry shunter based at Eastbourne. The last one was retrieved on 25 June. Consent to end all services from Polegate had been sought on 23 May, and with consent for extra buses to be run given on 15 August, the next day it was announced that the line would close on 8 September. On this day the service was run by DEMU No. 1112 but for the last two trips No. 1120 was added. Good crowds travelled on the last two trains and when the last return working reached Polegate at 22:40, the 'Cuckoo Line' had seen its last train.

While at Polegate, the direct line to Pevensey and Hastings by-passing Eastbourne had lost its only direct service, which had been the Sunday services from Ore to Victoria. Stone Cross Junction was then closed at night and during weekends, meaning all trains had to go via Eastbourne.

At nearby Uckfield, consent had been given to close the Uckfield–Lewes line as well as the short link between Ashurst Junction and Groombridge. The Minister of Transport had jumped the gun though. He had presumed that additional bus services between the two Sussex towns would simply be reliefs, but the Traffic Commissioners disagreed and convened a meeting that took place towards the end of November. After two days of submissions, the hearing was adjourned until the New Year. This meant that the line could not close, even though earth-moving equipment was ready on either side of the railway line. This gave BR a headache as a new timetable for the Oxted lines had been published and could not be altered. There was time within this new service to extend the service from Uckfield to Barcombe Mills, but not as far as Lewes. A shuttle service was introduced between the latter two, meaning that passengers had to change at Barcombe Mills. Closure of the line north of Uckfield was deferred but at the time it seemed that economies would be hard to come by, bearing in mind that the link to Lewes and Brighton had been cut. The Minister of Transport decided that there may be a case for retaining the section north of Uckfield on social and economic grounds. Clause 39 of the proposed Transport Bill allowed a social grant to be applied for, so the delay was to consider whether the grant would be value for money. Part of the reason for allowing the closure of the line south of Uckfield was that the intended Lewes relief road would no longer incur the expense of crossing the railway line.

Miscellanea

In 1968, an Act of Parliament separated the shipping interests of British Rail into a new division, for which the marketing name Sealink was adopted in 1970.

A new cross-Channel passenger service was inaugurated on 25 May between Folkestone and Ostende. The service was operated by Belgian Marine, but the SR co-operated by providing a rail connection to and from London. Dover Marine was becoming overcrowded and it was hoped that the new service would attract an increase in the 800,000 passengers per year already using the port. A new Customs and Immigration Hall was opened to coincide with the first sailing.

A new Hoverspeed service was launched between Portsmouth and Ryde using the new HM2 hovercraft. Journey time was 10–12 minutes and cost 1/6d (7½p) more than a ferry crossing.

The value of an alternative route from Brighton–London was evident on Sundays in February when work was being carried out in Balcombe Tunnel and all trains between the two went via Lewes and Uckfield. DEMUs were borrowed from Fratton but a Hastings six-car unit as well as loco-hauled stock were also needed.

The two motor coaches and two other coaches that were undamaged in the Hither Green accident in 1967 were used to form a four-car DEMU.

The eleven buffet cars in the 4-REP units were given names. These were not painted on the exterior but on glass panels behind the counter. The names were all places in the Southern area and included The Bournemouth, The Waterloo and The Solent.

Since the end of steam operations, withdrawn engines had been towed to scrap yards in South Wales. The last engines to leave Salisbury was on 30 March and were Nos 34034/102/35023/73035 bound for Buttigieg's of Newport.

Steam put in a brief appearance in April when Nos 75029 and 92203 ran under their own steam from Cricklewood–Liss en route to the Longmoor Military Railway.

B4 No. 30096 was still in steam and could be seen shunting at Corrall's yard at Southampton.

The start of the Channel Island tomato season still warranted two daily freights. Much traffic that used to dock at Southampton now arrived at Weymouth. At the height of the season, four trains were needed on a daily basis, with destinations of Water Orton and Crewe.

By May, Nine Elms shed was becoming unrecognisable. The large concrete coaling tower had been demolished as had the original London & Southampton Railway station on Nine Elms Lane. At the end of July, Nine Elms goods yard closed, with freight being transferred to the adjoining Western Region yard of South Lambeth, which was renamed Nine Elms (South Lambeth).

More stock was appearing in the new blue/grey livery including Pullman cars, which were losing their traditionally brown/cream colours. Some stock was still being repainted in varnished green livery with full yellow ends – 4-SUB No. 4118 was one such unit painted in August. As 4-VEPs were being repainted blue/grey from all-over blue, they were losing their raised aluminium logos in favour of painted ones.

The first of the Brighton Belle units, No. 3052, appeared in the blue/grey livery on the 09:25 Brighton–Victoria on 23 December. The Pullmans had lost their names and had 'Brighton Belle' substituted on the waistline of the carriages.

Steam reappeared at Brighton during June. *Oh! What a Lovely War* was being filmed and M7 No. 30245 had been brought from the Pullman Works and repainted on one side in LSWR colours and numbered 245. Smoke was seen emanating from the chimney but this was being produced by a device in the smokebox. All movements from the train were powered by an 'off-stage' diesel shunter.

In June and July there was a work-to-rule by railmen that caused disruption across the region. Signalmen and crossing keepers were put onto a two-shift system, which meant Sunday services were suspended and all lines closed between 22:00 and 06:00, resulting in newspapers having to be delivered by road. Road users were also inconvenienced by many level crossings remaining closed. Southampton boat trains were replaced by fleets of coaches and vans.

A cheap day excursion was run from Richmond and Staines to Bognor Regis on 21 August. It cost 10/- (50p) and needed two trains to cater for the 2,300 tickets sold.

With the end of steam, the decision was made to drop the prefix 'D' in front of diesel numbers as there was now no risk of confusion. Electric locos kept their 'E'.

Floods during September brought widespread disruption across the region. A bridge over the River Mole near Cobham was washed away and the viaduct just east of Godalming station collapsed under the force of the River Wey. A temporary bridge was constructed to allow single line working but this took two weeks to build. Fast services to Portsmouth were normally diverted via the Mid-Sussex line but the River Arun had burst its banks, causing flooding near Pulborough, and there had been a major landslip at Ockley. The disruption was so bad and widespread that the arrivals board at Waterloo remained blank for ten days.

Further east did not escape the deluge and flooding in Balcombe Tunnel closed the Brighton line on 15 September. Buses provided a link between Haywards Heath and Three Bridges and the alternative route via Uckfield and Oxted proved its worth, with one of the trains using it being the Newhaven boat train. East Grinstead could not be reached because of a landslip between Hurst Green and Lingfield. The Quarry line was closed in the afternoon because of floods near Earlswood and soon afterwards the Up Redhill line was blocked by a landslip near Merstham Tunnel. Numerous other lines were also affected.

One of the trains more adversely affected was the 08:40 Charing Cross to Hastings. It was diverted via Redhill and reached Edenbridge at about 10:45, only to find its route blocked by the River Medway bursting its banks, causing floods that put the power box at Tonbridge out of action. Before it could return to Redhill, the line became blocked behind it at Bletchingley tunnel, leaving the train stranded. A helicopter was called to rescue the stranded passengers, but poor visibility made it impossible for it to land. It was after dark before a bus managed to get close enough for the passengers to walk to. It took them to Edenbridge station from where they were able to join trains to Tunbridge Wells or Lewes and thence catch connections to Hastings, where they arrived just before midnight. Disruption of varying degrees continued for the next couple of weeks, with engineering works renewing damaged sections of track.

BR wished to demolish what is regarded as the oldest railway bridge in the world on the Canterbury & Whitstable Railway over Old Bridge Road. The Minister of Housing and Local Government said he would transfer the bridge from the supplementary list to the statutory list of buildings of special architectural or historic interest at the next revision, and suggested the local council could make a contribution to its repair. BR stated they could not wait that long and the bridge was demolished on 19 May 1969. Many locals and enthusiasts witnessed the demolition and took bricks away as souvenirs.

The 4-LAVs were fast being replaced by the new 4-VEPs, Nos 7721–55, on the Brighton line but six still survived towards the end of the year. The last unit of the new batch of 4-VEPs, No. 7755, had been delivered and an order for more was in place to replace the 2-BILs.

The three electric locomotives introduced during the 1940s were all withdrawn during the year. The last of the trio, No. 20003, introduced in 1948, was the first to go, being withdrawn in September and put in store at Brighton, while the two 1941 locos, Nos 20001 and 20002, were reportedly withdrawn in November, but No. 20001 worked an excursion over the direct Polegate–Stone Cross line on 4 January 1969.

With the introduction of the winter timetable, many marshalling yards throughout the region closed, the biggest of which was Three Bridges. The Up yard had been taken over by the Civil Engineer. He also took over the engine shed and yard.

No. E6018 passes through Eastleigh on a Bournemouth–Waterloo service on 1 July. (Courtesy Robert Carroll)

Electric locomotive No. 20001 in blue livery and double arrow logo at Brighton on 8 June. (Courtesy Robert Carroll)

The Golden Arrow passes Orpington in the hands of No. E50XX on 12 May. (Courtesy Robert Carroll)

A Class 74 electro-diesel, No. E6109, about to couple up to the Waterloo–Reina Del Mar boat train on 20 June.

An unusual shot in more ways than one. A Hastings six-car unit, No. 1034, passes through Barcombe Mills on 13 October with a boat train. The diversion was due to work being carried out in Balcombe Tunnel. (Courtesy Edwin Wilmshurst)

Two views of the same train with Class 33 No. D6557 pulling Stanier 2-6-4T No. 42500 to Brighton for storage in the old Pullman sheds. These photographs were taken on a dreary 7 December at Gatwick Airport. (Courtesy Edwin Wilmshurst)

2-BIL No. 2013 leaves Worthing Central heading for West Worthing on 2 November. (Courtesy Edwin Wilmshurst)

Chapter 10

1969

Service Levels

The Southern called a press conference at the start of the year to answer criticisms of their services from a number of complainants, including Parliament. Mr Lance Ibbotson, the General Manager, reviewed past performance and laid out plans for the future. He stressed that there was no scope for increasing services. He stated that timekeeping in 1968 had been disrupted by four major events that had long-lasting effects: the 25 mph speed limit at Hither Green following the fatal accident; the rebuilding of the Brighton line bridge at Battersea over the main lines to Waterloo; strikes by both rail unions through the summer months; and serious floods during September. Staff shortages were also blamed, with 112 guards and 120 signalmen needed on the Central Division alone.

It may be interesting to note the reasons for delays compared to those published post privatisation:

Train crews shortage	1.1 per cent
Train defects	1.4 per cent
Late arrivals from other regions	2.4 per cent
Abnormal speed restrictions	8.3 per cent
Station delays (including connections)	15.5 per cent
Incidents (inc. track/signal failures)	16.9 per cent
Reaction (cancellations/delays)	46.2 per cent
Reaction (late starts caused by late arrivals)	8.2 per cent

Ibbotson went on to say that over the next four years, £21 million was to be spent on new stock, £14 million on engineering works, £6 million on new track and £5 million on new colour light signals. The new stock would replace all pre-war stock that included 2-BIL, 2-HAL, 4-COR, 4-BUF and 4-GRI units. Fifty 4-VEP units had already been delivered and 111 4-CIGS were on order.

From 1 January some uneconomic, but socially desirable, services were to be subsidised by the government. They were to be awarded grants under Section 39 of the Transport Act 1968. These grants were allotted to 135 services nationwide, of which only a few were on the Southern. These were Ore–Brighton,

Brighton–Portsmouth, Portsmouth–Fareham, Eastleigh–Southampton–Salisbury, and Ryde–Shanklin.

Accidents

At Marden on 4 January in thick fog, the 20:00 Charing Cross–Ramsgate express, No. 7117/81, crashed into the rear of a parcels train pulling away from a signal check. The driver of the express and four passengers were killed and ten other passengers were taken to hospital.

The parcels train, which should have been 20 minutes in front of the express, had been held up by a special rail train limited to 25 mph. The second man of the parcels train had contacted the signalman to find out what the problem was as they had been held at two signals and he was told that there had been a problem previously with a short-circuit sending a signal to red and of the slow-running train in front of him and to phone again from Signal A 370. He did this even though the signal was at caution. He was told that the signal problem had been cleared and he could proceed normally. It was while pulling away from this signal that they were hit from behind. The leading carriage of No. 7117 finished up on its roof down an embankment 120 yards past the point of collision, while the second coach stopped on its side in front of the first coach. The third coach jack-knifed while the last five remained upright. The last three vans of the parcels train were totally destroyed. The driver of the express was blamed and, as he could not be quizzed, it was concluded that he had lost concentration and missed one signal at caution and the next at danger. Where his body was found would indicate that he saw the parcel train at the last moment, applied his brakes and then tried to retreat to a safer place.

On 7 January, Class 33, No. D6758 derailed in Clapham Junction sidings, causing three trains on the Windsor local lines to be cancelled.

May was not a good month at Eastleigh. On the 4th, a Class 73, No. E6028, became derailed while working the 18:25 Waterloo–Weymouth, blocking the line to St Denys and Portsmouth. On 25 May, at 07:35, a 4-TC unit derailed at the entrance to the carriage sidings at Eastleigh.

On 12 May, two PMVs that formed part of the morning paper train derailed just west of Paddock Wood, destroying around 100 yards of track. No. D6569 brought the breakdown crane from Ashford. The Up line that was partially blocked was cleared in time for the morning rush hour and the Down line cleared in time for the evening rush.

On 15 May, the 13:01 Brighton–Temple Mills freight pulled by No. D6574 suffered a derailment just south of Balham. Two Vanfits jumped the track and collided with the 15:36 Victoria–Bognor passenger train made up of 2-BILs and 2-HAPs. 2-BIl No. 2080 was badly damaged and 2-HAL No. 2696 less so. Services were badly affected for the rest of the day.

Eastleigh's breakdown crane became derailed on 27 September when it was being taken to Wandsworth to help with bridge reconstruction. It came off the rails at Hampton Court Junction when crossing from the local to the through line, causing major disruption to all services for the rest of the day.

On 5 December an accident occurred with a rake of empty coaches. It had been the 10:15 Exeter (St Davids) to Waterloo, arriving at Platform 14 with its locomotive at the buffers. In order to release the loco, No. D807 attached to the other end and drew the train forward to the Down Windsor Line and released the loco to Stewarts Lane shed. This was normal practice. The signalman then operated two shunting signals (224 and 227) so the train could be propelled back into Platform 14, ready to work the 15:10 Waterloo–Exeter. Unfortunately, he pulled 228 instead of 227, which operated a point. The train set back into Platform 12 and collided with a train of vans standing at the platform, derailing seven of them. One of these finished up leaning against 4-REP No. 3010, waiting to leave for Weymouth at 14:30. Prime responsibility for the accident lay with the shunter (who was riding in one of the carriages), for not noticing the second signal was at danger, although in his defence it was stated that due to the curvature of the track he could not see the signal and keep in contact with the train crew. The accident report made the point that this difficulty, which was well known at the station, had not been reported in writing. The train crew were also criticised for not keeping an adequate lookout on where their train was going and the signalman was also partially to blame for operating the wrong lever.

On Christmas Eve at Streatham Hill, two empty electric units collided, putting both running lines and access to the sheds out of action.

A week later at the same location a guard was killed when his van, which was part of a breakdown crane, was hit by 4-EPB No. 5167, which was being shunted.

Loco Movements

On 25 January there was an FA Cup tie between Southampton *v*. Aston Villa and three football specials were laid on. The last of these leaving Birmingham at 10:50 was a Blue Pullman and it was believed to be the first time one of these had ventured over Southern metals. It was serviced at Bournemouth before operating the return journey.

As the Class 74 electro-diesels came on line, the on-loan Class 47s were returned. Sending these back to be somewhat premature as the 74s were proving to be very unreliable. At one time in March only three were available out of the eight needed.

In April, Brighton Belle unit No. 3051 was returned from Eastleigh after being overhauled and repainted and it was paired with No. 3052 to work the first ten-car blue/grey Brighton Belle.

The first Hastings DEMUs to work into Southampton Docks was a twelve-car special from Pevensey & Westham to Southampton Eastern Docks (Ocean Terminal) on an educational visit to the *QE2*.

The Royal Train to the Derby was diesel-hauled for the first time. The carriages of this train were still steam-heated and the Southern had no locomotives capable of heating them, so a gleaming Type 2 still in green livery, No. D5518, was borrowed from the Eastern Region. The loco was used again on 15 July, when it headed a special carrying the President of Finland from Gatwick to Victoria.

Two specials were run by Bingo clubs taking players from Kent to Blackpool. Both trains were hauled by Class 33s as far as Willesden, where Nos E3081 and E3104 took them as far as Crewe. Nos D445 and D317 then took the trains to their destination.

The Class 74s were cleared to work fast freight trains, although their unreliability continued throughout the year and in December their availability was as low as two or three.

On 10 January two steam engines arrived from Lostock Hall. No. 75027 was towed to Haywards Heath before being moved to the Bluebell Railway, and No. 45110 went to Ashford Works.

Line Closures

The removal of freight services from Blandford Forum on 6 January meant the former S&D line south of Templecombe had now closed.

The trams on Ryde Pier were withdrawn from 27 January but additional trains were run from the pier head to Ryde Esplanade, with the empty stock running to Ryde St John's Road where it crossed over to return for another journey.

The direct line from Polegate–Pevensey and Westham closed on 6 January. This and the closure of the branch to Hailsham and the extensive goods yard reduced Polegate to a simple two-road station, which enabled the station to be moved back to the original site adjacent to the town's main shopping street. This loop line, as it was known locally, stayed open for engineers' trains only. Permission had to be granted to enter or leave the main line. The track between Hailsham and Polegate was lifted from April, bringing the materials to Polegate using the contractor's Trackmobile tractor. This left the section between Heathfield and Hailsham still in place and isolated, so it had to be removed by road.

The sidings at Polegate began to be used as storage roads for condemned EMUs awaiting scrapping and stacks of track sections lifted from the Hailsham line. It was thought that these were being stored prior to removal to the Gypsum Mines at Robertsbridge, where their sidings were being replaced and extended. The condemned stock had been cleared by mid-August.

Following on from the Uckfield debacle in the 1968 section, the Traffic Commissioners met again on 20 January for two days to consider bus licensing but still could not reach a decision and adjourned the meeting. British Rail said that due to the serious state of the viaduct in Lewes, it would close the line anyway, and, if necessary, run a bus service as it held a licence to operate between all stations.

The last trains actually ran on 23 February with DEMU No. 1318 working the section south of Barcombe Mills, with the last trips being the 20:40 Lewes–Barcombe Mills and the 21:00 return trip, while No. 1301 worked the 19:58 Tunbridge Wells–Barcombe Mills and the 20:51 Barcombe Mills–Oxted. British Rail did run their own replacement bus service. The stations at Barcombe Mills and Isfield stayed open for the sale of rail tickets that were available for use on the replacement buses. These buses were too big for the country lane leading to Barcombe Mills station so a minibus or taxis were needed to take passengers to the replacement bus that stopped on the A26. The Traffic Commissioners were still refusing to licence a replacement bus service run by other operators.

The saga concluded in April with an announcement that BR's bus service would finish in May and an hourly bus service between Lewes and Uckfield would be run (reluctantly) by Southdown, who expected to make a loss of £19,000 p.a. operating it. These replacement bus services no longer had to be subsidised by BR. It was regretted that the Minister did not change his mind and authorise a social grant for a re-laid Hamsey loop following the original line, thus keeping the line and alternative route between the south coast and the Capital open – an idea that is still proposed today.

Permission was granted to close the Swanage branch, although no date was given. Swanage and Corfe Castle stations would close, but the line would stay open as far as Furzebrook Sidings for the clay traffic. Surprise was expressed locally at the hasty decision, as there had not been enough time to assess any possible upturn in trade caused by the electrification of the main line.

The closure of the Swanage branch that was scheduled for 6 October was postponed because the replacement bus licences had not been issued. Through trains to Waterloo were stopped from this date, with all journeys over the line were worked by a single DEMU.

Notices were posted for the closure of the Hastings–Ashford line. On 25 November the Hastings–Ashford Line Closure Protest Committee chartered a six-car DEMU, which called at all stations on the line before running non-stop to Charing Cross.

Miscellanea

Feltham marshalling yard closed on 6 January when a new freight timetable was introduced.

In the summer timetable, the Walsall–Eastbourne service was discontinued, which meant there were now no through trains from the Midlands to the Sussex coast.

In January, motormen in South London were unhappy about rest-day workings and were operating an overtime ban and lightning strikes, leading to delays and cancellations on commuter lines from London Bridge.

Brighton Belle unit No. 3052, which had recently been renovated, was suffering frequent failures, and with No. 3051 being at Eastleigh for renovation, some services were being operated with a 5-BEL/4-COR formation. On 15 September, Brighton Belle unit No. 3051 caught fire in Brighton station. No one was injured but it was badly damaged, with one car being almost completely burnt out. The other two units were used for every subsequent trip with a 4-COR standing in should any of them become unavailable.

The last of the 4-LAVs were withdrawn in February. By February new 4-CEPs were beginning to replace the 2-BILs on the Brighton line and sidings at Gatwick were used to park some of the displaced stock. 4-CORs also took over the Brighton–Eastbourne–Hastings services, displacing even more 2-BILs.

At least ten 2-BIL and 2-HAP units have had their seats and heating removed and are being used as parcels trains. They were classified as 2-PARs.

No. 3001 was the first 4-REP to be painted in the blue/grey livery.

Blizzards during February caused widespread chaos. Many point heaters were being blown out, causing them to jam up. There were no de-icing trains on the Isle of Wight so any icing of conductor rails had to be left to nature to thaw out.

On 7 February the 21:36 Charing Cross–Ramsgate, made up of two 4-CEPs, Nos 7107/7201, got stuck in a snowdrift between Herne Bay and Reculver. The driver could not back up and try another run at the drift because a drift had also built up behind him. When the guard got out to lay detonators, he found himself up to his waist in snow. The air-sea rescue helicopter was asked if they could rescue the stranded passengers, but they were told the chopper could not land until dawn. The nearest road, the A2, was over a mile away. Eventually, at 07:03, Nos E6036 and D6596 arrived and pulled the EMUs with their seven passengers back to Herne Bay.

£14 million was spent during 1969 on renewing 235 miles of track, including laying 142 miles of welded rail. In 1961 there were only 33 miles throughout the region but this had gradually increased and by the end of the decade there were nearly 800 miles.

Some of the 56XX Class of 2-HAPs were converted to second-class only and reclassified as 2-SAPs. The first to be treated was No. 5607.

Earlier reports on the 8-VAB unit suggested that it could not be split but these were proved wrong on 11 April when, while working the 11:47 Waterloo–Bournemouth, it arrived at Basingstoke suffering with some hot wheels. Three carriages were detached and it continued with five coaches, which included two driving trailers.

A fire broke out on Folkestone Harbour station on 22 April, damaging the buffet and a wooden platform. Boat trains were terminated at Folkestone Central station and passengers had to be taken to the ferries by bus.

Her Majesty attended the NATO review at Spithead on 16 May, but travelled by service train – the 09:50 Waterloo–Portsmouth – but the normal 4-COR/4-BUF stock was replaced by newly painted blue/grey 4-CIGs/4-BIG Nos 7318/7037/7324.

A third freightliner train was introduced from the Millbrook Depot. This was the 22.40 SX to Garston, returning at 20.15 SX from Garston.

An excursion from Bedford failed at Faversham Junction during June. It blocked the Up Ramsgate and Down Dover lines as well as the line from the shed line where No. E6017 was available and could have rescued it. Investigations found out that the loco had run out of fuel even though the gauge stated there was still 650 gallons in the tank.

There was an unofficial strike by signalmen on the South Western Division during July. Signalmen at the panel box at Eastleigh and seven or eight mechanical boxes in the Southampton area walked out causing many trains to be cancelled. The Central Division didn't escape the strike and 10 July saw the most widespread action with many signalmen failing to turn up for work. Disruption varied, with Eastbourne being the worst hit and no trains getting any closer than Lewes. Redhill station was closed but the Quarry Line remained open. The chaos continued when drivers from London Bridge and other depots walked out over a roster dispute on 4 August. Suburban services were badly affected but some express journeys ran using drivers from other depots. Another dispute arose with diesel drivers from Norwood striking against locos being worked through from other regions, as those men were being paid a mileage bonus. This not only affected freight traffic but also some Oxted line passenger services.

Another lightning strike occurred on the afternoon of 4 August when twenty motormen based at South London depots walked out.

The Newhaven–Stirling Motorail service was unique in that it was the only passenger service to pass through all BR regions. It was also the only passenger service to cover freight-only lines as it wound its way through West London, and was the only regular working for a Class 45 on the Central Division. 1969 was to be the last year that this service operated.

The first automatic barriers at a station car cark were installed at Staplehurst on 2 June. Entrance was unobstructed but on leaving, a 2/- (10p) coin or season ticket had to be inserted in order to raise the barrier to exit. Unfortunately, it broke down on the first evening, leaving a lot of trapped commuters.

The Isle of Wight pop festival was held at the end of August and ten special trains were run from Waterloo–Portsmouth Harbour, with nineteen return trains. No damage was reported, unlike the 4-TC that was badly damaged by Chelsea fans returning from Southampton.

A new ferry was delivered for service between Portsmouth and Fishbourne. It was a 700-ton roll on/roll off vessel, MV *Cuthred*, built by Richards (Shipbuilders) Ltd of Lowestoft. It was capable of carrying forty-eight cars and 400 passengers on the 45-minute crossing. It would be an addition to the two ferries already in use on the route. The number of vehicles carried to the island had increased from 125,000 in 1960 to 298,000 in 1967.

Since the closure of the Uckfield–Lewes line, DEMUs on the Oxted lines now have to reach their servicing centre at St Leonards via Haywards Heath, Lewes and Eastbourne.

On 5 July an excursion was run to the last open day at Longmoor. The nine-coach train was met at Liss Junction by 2-10-0 *Gordon* already attached to five coaches and the fourteen-coach train set off for Longmoor.

2-BIL No. 2064 in blue livery with full yellow ends leaves Arundel with a Victoria–Bognor train on 8 June. (Courtesy Edwin Wilmshurst)

Green 2-BIL with full yellow ends faces up to a new 4-VEP at Barnham. (Courtesy Trevor Tupper)

Electric locomotive No. 20001 heads an LCGB tour *The Sussex Venturer* at Newhaven on 4 January. (Courtesy Edwin Wilmshurst)

Some 4-CORs ended their days on the Brighton–Ore via Eastbourne service. One such unit, No. 3140, was photographed at Lewes. (Courtesy John Law)

4-VEP No. 7774 in blue livery with aluminium logo at East Croydon on a Victoria–Redhill service. (Courtesy John Law)

The driver walks towards the cab of his deplorable looking 4-COR, No. 3139, at London Bridge (Courtesy John Law)

4-COR No. 4357 approaches Battersea Park on a Victoria–Bellingham service. (Courtesy John Law)

Approaching Willingdon Junction just outside Eastbourne with a Victoria service is 4-CIG No 7336.

2-HAL No. 2603, still in green livery with full yellow front, passes Gatwick Airport on 7 April. (Courtesy Robert Carroll)

Another 2-HAL but in rail blue with double arrow insignia at Lewes. (Courtesy Robert Carroll)

4-COR No. 3103 passes
Southwick on a London
Bridge–Littlehampton
via the Quarry Line and
Worthing service. (Courtesy
Robert Carroll)

4-SUB No. 4742 passes
a redundant water tower
at Beckenham Junction.
(Courtesy Robert Carroll)

With Lovers Walk sheds
in the background, 2-HAL
No. 2685 enters Brighton.
(Courtesy Robert Carroll)

4-EPB No. 5017 at Forest Hill on 8 February. (Courtesy Robert Carroll)

2-BIL No. 2025 in blue livery passing Shoreham. (Courtesy Robert Carroll)

Still in green livery, 2-HAP unit No. 6009 passes Petts Wood on 16 August. (Courtesy Robert Carroll)

4-VEP No. 7713 in original livery in a cutting near Patcham. It was unusual to see one from this batch on the Brighton line in 1969. (Courtesy Robert Carroll)

Summary

The 1960s had been a decade of change on the railways. For some, the changes had been good. Dirty, smelly steam engines had been replaced by smart, modern, clean diesel or electric multiple units. I daresay that even some railwaymen appreciated the cleaner, less arduous working conditions.

For many, though, it was the end of an era. The last of the living, breathing, noisy steam engines had disappeared, along with most of the hoards or schoolboys and older trainspotters waiting on the ends of platforms throughout the country. Many of the engine sheds, which were once atmospheric Victorian buildings, fell into disrepair before being demolished to make way for car parks, shopping centres or housing estates.

For some communities though, it was more serious. They were left without a railway service. Beeching had closed many rural lines, forcing rail users to find alternative means of transport: for the less fortunate this meant a longer, slower bus ride, but many purchased their first car or motorcycle and the railways lost their patronage forever.

Another result of branch line closures was the loss of alternative routes between large population centres. This is aptly demonstrated by the Brighton line. All services from Brighton and Eastbourne to London now have to go over the Ouse Valley Viaduct, which is now well over 150 years old. With the line between Lewes and Uckfield lifted and the line between Haywards Heath and East Grinstead now owned mainly by the Bluebell Railway, any serious problems with the viaduct will have a massive impact on travellers.

Although there will be further changes in the future, including the privatisation of services, I doubt they will have the same impact that the changes in the 1960s did.